MARKET PLACE MINISTERS

**AWAKENING GOD'S PEOPLE IN THE WORKPLACE
TO THEIR ULTIMATE PURPOSE**

PAUL GAZELKA

**CREATION
HOUSE PRESS**

MARKETPLACE MINISTERS by Paul Gazelka
Published by Creation House Press
A part of Strang Communications Company
600 Rinehart Road
Lake Mary, FL 32746
www.creationhouse.com

Unless otherwise noted, scriptures quoted are from the New American Standard version of the Bible. Copyright © 1960, 1962, 1963, 1968, 1971, 1972, 1973, 1975, 1977 by the Lockman Foundation. Used by permission.

Scripture quotations marked NKJV are from the New King James Version of the Bible. Copyright © 1979, 1980, 1982 by Thomas Nelson, Inc., publishers. Used by permission.

Cover design by Terry Clifton
Interior design by David Bilby

Library of Congress Control Number: 2002116059
International Standard Book Number: 0-88419-978-9

03 04 05 06   8 7 6 5 4 3 2 1
Printed in the United States of America.

To Contact the Author:

Paul Gazelka
15229 Edgewood Drive
Baxter, Minnesota 56425
E-mail: paul.gazelka.g8ym@statefarm.com
E-mail: mrandmrs@uslink.net
Phone: (800) 269-9694
Fax: (218) 829-9545

Acknowledgments

God has used significant relationships with people to bring me to where I am today.

My wife, Maralee, completes me. Twenty years of marriage to a woman with Christian values similar to mine has been the greatest gift I could ever have asked of the Lord. Maralee, you always encourage me to pursue God's highest plan for my life. You were the first one to encourage me to move from talking about this book to actually writing it. Thank you, my dearest love.

Thanks, Mom and Dad, Gene and Joyce Gazelka. You fulfilled the Lord's mandate to parents to raise godly children. By first representing Christ in our home, you showed us by your example how to represent Christ in the world. We never wondered if you loved us. We never wondered if you loved God. It wasn't religion you modeled for us; it was a personal relationship with Jesus Christ.

Regarding this book, I appreciate the encouragement I received from Phil Derstine, John Kelly, Mark Gorman, Rich Marshall, Dennis and Megan Doyle, Steve Strang, Al Lindner, Harold Eatmon, Brian Gazelka, Russ Kalenberg, Peter Wagner, Millie Bertilson, David Cartledge and others. God used all of you in one way or another to help me complete this book.

Contents

Introduction

*I*t was midnight. I was on a business trip with my wife, Maralee. I couldn't sleep. I couldn't get it out of my mind that a Christian friend of mine who was in the same organization I was had been caught having an affair. He knew better.

We were staying at the same hotel, but he was not with his wife. He was alone.

The Lord impressed upon my wife and me that I should call him and challenge him to keep his covenant marriage vows.

"I'm not sure I love her," he said.

"You know you do," I answered.

He eventually reconciled with his wife.

The Lord has given me influence in my profession, both with my peers and my clients. I'm an insurance agent—but so much more.

Turn another few pages of my life, and you will find me in Peru with my wife and children. We were invited by pastors Guillermo and Milagros Aguayo from Camino Lavida Church to come to Lima and minister at churches.

It was an awesome time of ministry. God put us before Peruvian National politicians and musicians, as well as everyday people, to share biblical truths on marriage, family and finances. They introduced me as Pastor Paul Gazelka from Minnesota.

I found that a little strange because I don't pastor an organized church body. Even so, as we went, I felt the authority of a five-fold ministry upon us. (See Ephesians 4:10–12.) After one of my messages for men, more than two hundred men came forward to repent of sexual sins. It was exciting to see God use me in that capacity.

A few months later, I convened an annual men's conference that drew attendees from thirty churches.

Pastor Russ Kalenberg shared how God had put him and his wife on the CBS television show *The Amazing Race*. Joe Zupetz taught about the importance of worship for men. Pastor Phil Derstine shared how God had opened doors for him to minister at Ground Zero in New York City just after 9/11.

I shared a message on the very subject of this book, *Marketplace Ministers*. It was a powerful weekend.

Then Monday morning came, and I opened the doors of my insurance agency for business. Through my insurance business alone, I interact with almost two thousand families. I don't just talk about insurance; I relate with my customers on a spiritual level as well.

In times of calamity, they come to see me. If a client has lost a loved one, he calls on me because I wrote the life-insurance policy for that person. If someone has lost her house due to a storm or a fire, she sees me because I wrote the home insurance. God has put me in a strategic position to provide compassion and care for people in a variety of situations.

You see, I am a "marketplace minister." The marketplace for me happens to be in the financial service industry, but for you, it is wherever God has placed you in an occupation.

I am called to ministry, but I am also called to the marketplace. God has raised me up to be a person of influence for His kingdom outside the conventional church walls. In this way, I rub shoulders with people from all walks of life.

He has also called me to minister within the traditional church walls, teaching and equipping fellow saints. It took me a long time to figure out that being in both roles not only was OK in God's eyes, but it also was actually very good in His view.

That's what this book is all about: defining who a marketplace minister is, what he or she does, and releasing him or her into their fullest calling in Christ. When you see what God has destined you to be, you can run the race set before you with joy and confidence.

God is doing a new work in the earth today. He is accomplishing His purpose, not just through those He has called into conventional full-time ministry roles, but also through people whom He has called while remaining in their professional trade. He wants to maximize their usefulness and influence for His kingdom through their vocational calling.

The apostle Paul is a biblical example of this combination of secular work and ministry. When he was well into his apostleship, he still operated his trade of tent-making as a way to provide his own needs. (See

Acts 18:3; 20:34; 1 Corinthians 9.) He clearly encouraged ministers to receive their physical or monetary compensation from the work of spreading the gospel, but at times during his ministry, he chose not to.

In no way do I want to minimize the current role of the pastor or other professional ministers—those paid for their work in ministry. They are vital to the plan of God for helping to fulfill the Great Commission, but they clearly can't do it alone.

I want to raise the level of importance of the marketplace ministers, those destined for ministry in the marketplace. Many of these ministers will be compensated through their occupations rather than by the gospel they are reflecting every day.

Why? Because God has other ways for ministers to make their livelihood than strictly from ministry. The overarching issue is not money and occupation. It is simply this: Are we doing what God has called us to do?

Being in the marketplace has more to do with going out into the "highways and byways" and inviting the lost to the King's wedding feast. (See Matthew 22:1–10). Our highways and byways are unique to us and our occupations.

More important than inviting them to church with us is inviting them to have a personal relationship with their Creator. Finding a good church is secondary.

How many of the people we see in our occupations (or, our "flock") would never set foot in church? Too many to count! And if they won't come to our churches, doesn't that leave us and others like us as their only "contact" with the Heavenly Father?

We live in perilous, changing, exciting times, when people from all walks of life are desperately looking for the meaning of life. We have the only answer to their hearts' cry: Jesus Christ.

Being in the marketplace is not just about raising resources for the kingdom of God through our work. It's also about being people of influence for God's kingdom-purposes through our work. As we grow and mature as believers, and as we become success-ful in what we put our hands to do, our opportunities for influence multiply.

Chapter one through chapter four of this book contain my personal testimony—how I learned to be comfortable with my calling in both the marketplace and ministry. You will find helpful insights through-out these four chapters that I have learned simply by traveling the road of life.

From chapter five to the end I define *marketplace ministers* and some common misconceptions about them. I also identify some qualities necessary to be influential in the marketplace. Then I take some time to address the subject of wealth—its purpose, and how to increase it and effectively use it for the king-dom of God. Finally, I address a godly strategy for reaping the End-Times harvest.

Are you a marketplace minister? I trust God will bring you clarity and that He will answer this ques-tion for you as you read this book. I hope you will enjoy reading it as much as I have enjoyed writing it.

PART ONE: TESTIMONY

Chapter One

THE BEGINNING
OF THE CALL

*B*ack in 1975 I was a tall, lanky, "trying to look cool" fifteen-year-old, working my way through adolescence. I came from a typically large Roman Catholic family of ten children. I was the fifth-oldest child.

A few years earlier, God began to awaken our family to the third person of the Trinity, the Holy Spirit. In the summer of 1975 we attended a Lutheran conference on the Holy Spirit in Minneapolis, Minnesota. I've never been the same since.

I was spiritually hungry and wanted to be filled with the Holy Spirit, and God emphatically answered that request. That was the beginning of learning to be led by the Holy Spirit. I no longer attend the Catholic Church. However, I'm thankful God isn't interested in denominational labels but hungry hearts that will respond to His grace.

My encounter with the Holy Spirit also is important because of another significant event in my life that happened the same year. At age fifteen, to become an insurance agent with a specific company was already on my heart.

What fifteen-year-old dreams of being an insurance agent? I can understand if a boy wants to become something glamorous, such as an astronaut or fireman...but an insurance agent?

What movie or television show have you ever seen that depicts an insurance agent as being cool? In the movie *Groundhog Day* the star character, acted by Bill Murray, has to continue to relive Groundhog Day until he gets it right. Every day he sees the same characters over and over and over.

One of the characters is an insurance agent. He's pushy, obnoxious and loud. The main character can't get away from him. The day is like hell, and the agent is part of the nightmare until Murray lives the day as he should.

Insurance agents generally are not thought of very highly. When people are asked what they think of the profession, it is ranked among the least-liked. Who would dream of being an insurance agent at age fifteen? Only the Spirit of God would have put that desire in me.

It was more than coincidence that during that same year I was filled with the Holy Spirit, I acquired the dream of becoming an insurance agent. I can say now that the vocational desire was the leading of the Holy Spirit. It became my goal, and is still part of what I do today.

As a point of clarification, I should mention that my dad also was in the insurance profession and very active in ministry. He modeled what I would become. I have no doubt that just wanting to be like him influenced my own desires, though the timing of when I became interested in the profession is still significant.

God wants to orchestrate our lives, combining all of our individual gifts, talents and experiences into a grand purpose. Jeremiah 29:11 declares that God knows the plans He has for us—plans to prosper us and not to harm us, plans to give us a future and hope. The Lord has a unique individual plan for each of us.

SEEKING GOD'S PLAN FOR MY LIFE

I graduated from high school and set off to college to earn my degree in business. Getting a business degree was always my goal, but I wandered through a few colleges to obtain it.

I started at the University of Minnesota-Duluth. I wasn't very mature as a Christian yet, and found it difficult to live a victorious Christian life in the college setting. I had rededicated my life to the Lord just after graduating from high school, but I was still struggling with worldly desires.

I made a decision to transfer to a Christian college. But where that would be, I did not know. No one in my family had gone to a Christian college.

I found out one of my cousins was going to LeTourneau University in Longview, Texas. I prayed about going there, and I even fasted about that decision (a first for me). Finally, I felt peace that this was the Lord's direction.

LeTourneau was a Southern Baptist college and had a student population of several thousand. The denominational differences were unique enough, but the real struggle was the demographics of the student body: 90 percent men, 10 percent women. *Nine guys to one girl!* How could a single Christian man meet a single Christian woman in a place like that?

It could only be from God's hand, I surmised, and God's hand didn't have someone there for me. Just the same, it was a wonderful time and place for me to seek the Lord with all my heart.

I attended a nondenominational charismatic church named Rolling Hills. We called the pastor by his first name, so that's all I remember—Brother Stan.

I had great respect for him and looked to him for direction in my life. He delivered the Word of God in a way that left me hungry to come back for more. He opened his pulpit to prominent national Christian ministers who enlarged my vision of the body of Christ.

I became a passionate, on-fire believer. This marked the first time I wanted to have an impact on the world for Christ. My desire was no longer just about what was in it for me; I wanted to know what I could do for Jesus.

At LeTourneau was where the struggle began in my soul to discover and confirm what God really wanted me to do with my life. It's a struggle many men and women wrestle with all their lives. Some people are never sure that the decisions they make for daily living are ones that will truly please God.

As a general rule, I've discovered that if you are seeking the Lord first, typically what you are good at, and what you love to do, is part of God's plan for your life. Just do it!

At the time, I didn't have this revelation.

I was struggling with what appeared to be two opposite directions in life: the ministry and the marketplace. With my passion to serve Jesus, I assumed that the only path for me was "full-time" ministry, living financially from my work as a minister of the gospel.

I had two key questions burning in my heart:

- I was sold out for Jesus, so I probably should get my full living from the gospel, right?

- What about my desire to be a professional insurance agent? Was that six years of wasted thinking, or was it a seed of calling and direction from the heart of the Father God?

I was in a dilemma, and I didn't know what to do. This was an unusual situation for me. By temperament, I always knew what to do. On personality tests, I scored a high D—the choleric lion who knows what to do. Well, in this case, I didn't know what to do, and I didn't want to miss God's will for me.

There was a ministry up the road from LeTourneau called *Agape Force*. I had never met anyone from that ministry, but they worked with youth, and I was young, so I thought this might be the direction for me.

I was waiting for an audible voice from God, and He wasn't giving me one. My emotions were in turmoil, clouding the inward witness the Lord gives us for direction. I couldn't decide what to do, so I decided to visit Brother Stan.

I assumed that he, being the man of God he was, would see my passion to serve Jesus and confirm that I should leave my dream of being in the marketplace. He would tell me to answer the call for "full-time" ministry. After all, that's what pastors do—send you forth on mission trips or off to Bible schools, right?

Brother Stan didn't do that. He said to me, "God is looking for honest insurance agents, and that's what I think you should do."

His brief proclamation brought peace to my soul. I knew he had given me an answer from the heart of our Heavenly Father. I was back on the track God had laid before me years earlier.

An Early Lesson About Ministry

I transferred to Oral Roberts University (ORU) in Tulsa, Oklahoma, for my final year and a half of college. I would like to say that the Holy Spirit prompted me to go, and He may have, but the decision didn't appear that spiritual.

Remember how LeTourneau University was a place where nine in ten students were male? If you want to be a monk, that would be fine, but I didn't want to be one.

Some friends and I decided to take a spring-break trip to ORU. The administration provided a free weekend at the campus for prospective students who wanted to take a look at the school. We were simply looking for a free place to go over spring break.

Two things got my attention on that weekend getaway: the abundance of attractive Spirit-filled women and the strong presence of the Holy Spirit. Either one of those reasons is why I quickly decided to transfer to ORU and finish my business degree.

Attending Oral Roberts University for just one and a half years changed me. Oral Roberts' vision for the college was to graduate students in every field to go into every realm of life with the gospel of Jesus Christ. He understood the need for the gospel to be present in every sphere of influence, in every part of the marketplace.

I thrived at ORU. Being there solidified my career path for business and intensified my passion to serve Jesus.

Just after I made the decision to transfer to ORU and was accepted, I went home for summer break. Wouldn't you know it...I met the woman of my dreams, Maralee, back in my hometown of Virginia, Minnesota. So much for going to Oral Roberts University to get my "marriage" degree!

Maralee and I married the summer before my last half-year of college. We were in Tulsa together while I finished school.

We've been married for twenty years. I can't express strongly enough how important it has been for me to have married a woman with a like-minded passion to serve Jesus.

Sometimes we have whole-hearted disagreements, but it typically is about God's will in a matter, not something temporal. Proverbs 27:17 proclaims that as "iron sharpens iron, so one man sharpens another." Maralee sharpens my usefulness as a tool for the

Lord like no other person I know. I'm eternally grateful that the Lord has given her to me.

At Oral Roberts University, I had to work full time to cover my college expenses. During that time, Maralee and I worked in the evenings cleaning medical offices.

At the time, two of my brothers also lived in Tulsa while attending Bible school. We three brothers ended up working together cleaning the offices of an entire building.

We were the buffing crew, and we made it fun. Often one of us would work our way ahead and then find some dark corner from which to jump out when the others least expected it. It kept us on our toes.

Other Bible-college students also worked evenings cleaning the medical buildings, and it was during this time that I began to see that a great misunderstanding existed among Christians about so-called full-time ministry.

One evening I was talking with one of the college's Bible students, and he asked me what I would be doing after graduation. I told him with excitement about my plans to run my own insurance agency.

He shared with me that he was going into the "full-time ministry." He wasn't sure yet exactly what he would be doing, only that it would be "full time."

"I'm going into full-time ministry, too," I answered.

"No, you're not. You know what I mean," he responded.

I did know what he meant, but he didn't know what I meant.

As we conversed, I was troubled in my spirit. I was serving Jesus full time already. It was all I thought about. Was a calling to be in the marketplace not equal with receiving all my income from preaching the gospel? Was my concept of ministry less important to God?

It had begun to feel like it was.

I knew in my spirit that I was called to the marketplace, but I also felt very much called to ministry. Couldn't it be both? Seeds of doubt crept into my being; I wasn't sure anymore. Did I have to choose one over the other? To serve Jesus at the highest level, did I have to leave the marketplace before I even got there? I was disturbed in my spirit but continued on my determined path.

Chapter Two

In the Marketplace

After graduating from ORU, I began looking for work in my chosen profession of insurance. Maralee and I had saved $1,000 while in Tulsa, and with that abundant cache of money, we moved north to Minnesota.

Because I knew insurance sales with a specific company was my calling, I thought landing the job would come rather quickly. I was wrong. Both my parents and my in-laws lived within thirty minutes of one another, so we decided that we would stay with them until I secured the job.

After six months of interviewing with no success, and moving back and forth between Maralee's parents' house and my parents' house, my confidence and pride were gone. I can only imagine what my in-laws must have thought: *He promised our daughter the moon, and now they are moving in with us!*

We were down to our last one hundred dollars when we got the green light to take over an insurance agency. That was cutting it way too close for me.

The agency was in a small western Minnesota town that was far from anything familiar. Even so, we were excited and very grateful for the opportunity.

The agency manager who hired me had tried to

11

hire two older, more qualified individuals for this agency, but at the last minute each of them had backed out. The manager was desperate, so he took a chance on me. I was a very young twenty-three-year-old with no experience...but a lot of enthusiasm.

While interviewing for the position, the topic of where I graduated from college came up. The manager had been exposed to Christianity, but he didn't believe in Jesus as the Savior and the only way to heaven. He said as much in the interview.

As tactfully as I could, I disagreed with him. What could I say but the truth? Initially, I wasn't offered the job, and I felt certain that issue was one of the reasons.

Sometimes in the role as a *marketplace minister* God asks us to make a stand for the gospel that is not popular or accepted. We must be led of the Spirit, and we must be willing to make that stand. It could have cost me this opportunity. It didn't—but it could have.

In this case, the Lord kept the position for me.

My manager is now deceased. I attended his funeral and listened to the minister share he had wasted away in a nursing home during the last season of his life. The minister told how his independence had been lost with his illness and how, through that loss, my manager discovered he desperately needed Jesus as his Savior.

The minister had prayed with him to receive Jesus before he died. I can't help but believe that my personal testimony of Christ was part of what the Lord used to soften his heart over the years.

GOD'S WORK IN GOD'S WAY

In my insurance career, there has been nothing but success. Within the first few months of my new career, David Baker, a minister, offered to pray for my business endeavors. I agreed.

He told me to hold my wallet in my hands. Then he laid his hands over mine and prayed that the Lord would bless our business abundantly. In my first full year in the business, I was among the top fifty agents out of more than seven thousand agents nationwide. I continued to be one of the top fifty agents for the next five years.

God was prospering me. I worked very few nights in a profession that often seems to demand it for great success. God was putting the spotlight on me for promotion.

This stage of my career was typical of many Christians' careers in the marketplace. I was trying to be a good Christian man in the community. I was involved in leadership positions in the community, not for the kingdom of God, but rather as influence for my own "kingdom."

I was a regular church attendee and somewhat involved, but my heart was business first, ministry second. My wife often would be the first one to become involved in church ministry. Then I would get minimally involved.

I was open to being involved in ministry-related activities only if they did not interfere with or jeopardize my business activities. This represented a critical paradigm shift that needed to take place in my life which did not occur for another six years.

I needed a rearrangement of priorities. I had always known that in order of importance they were: 1) my personal relationship with the Lord; 2) my relationship with my wife; 3) my relationship with our children. The first three were set, but they weren't always in their proper order. It was my priorities after the first three that were clearly out of balance.

In my heart, I had placed work before ministry. God wanted to rearrange that. It wasn't that God didn't want me to do my job with excellence, but whenever He brought someone to me who needed to see or hear the gospel, I needed to respond. The Lord's work was the priority, come what may!

Luke 10:29-37 tells the story of a man being robbed on the side of the road and left to die. Religious people passed by, too busy to stop. A certain Samaritan who was on a journey, probably a business trip, saw the man and stopped to help him. He understood that ministry comes before marketplace activities. We need to be available to God in the same way.

TESTED IN PARIS

After five years, I desired to become a manager in the organization I worked for. Typically, only agents who had performed at superior levels—who had demonstrated they could relate well to everyone—were hired.

I had met the qualification of high performance, but would I be able to relate to agents who didn't share the same spiritual ideals that were important to me? For example, how would I relate to someone who consumed large amounts of alcohol or who had been married numerous times? Would I be able to lead and respect people with views different from mine? God expects us to.

I had been a candidate for promotion for about two years, and I was wondering why it had not yet happened.

Our church put on an annual camp meeting in which we could take a few days off to go to a retreat center and get recharged as believers. I remember walking by myself one starry night and asking the Lord if I would be a manager in northeast Minnesota. I remember the strong impression that came in response to my question.

"You will go north, but not as far north as you think," He had said.

A few months later a manager in northwest Minnesota announced his retirement. I was promoted to his position, and we moved five hours north of where we were living. The position I originally thought about in northeast Minnesota was six hours north, not five.

The company had some reservations about putting me in this particular location because I was very different from the retiring manager. He set up many social functions that provided alcoholic beverages, a role opposite my personal convictions. They wondered if I would be a good fit. Somehow I needed to establish that I was also a good leader, although different from my predecessor.

The opportunity to establish a new path of leadership happened during a company-sponsored trip to Paris. We were invited to a dinner function by the agency team we were about to oversee. We thought it was a great idea until the location of the dinner was given—the Moulin Rouge.

I vaguely remembered having heard of the Moulin Rouge; what I remembered wasn't good. Maralee also had a strong check in her spirit about this place, and she didn't want us to go. Our worst fears were confirmed: Topless dancers were the entertainment of the establishment.

What was I to do? I wanted the opportunity to meet this group of agents, but I certainly did not want to promote that kind of entertainment.

I called the Moulin Rouge to confirm the fact that there were topless dancers. The man who answered the phone spoke some English but not enough to understand exactly what I was asking him.

I had asked, "When does the dancing begin?" He responded in broken English that the dancing would begin after the dessert was served.

I suddenly came up with a great idea. We could go to the dinner, quickly eat our dessert and graciously leave before the dancers came out. My wife thought it was a lousy idea, but I pressured her into going along with it. At the time I didn't pay much attention to the gift God had placed within her to discern potential problems. I do now.

We had a wonderful dinner; we even did some

dancing to ballroom music. The time for dessert came. My plan worked beautifully up to that point. It ended when the dessert came out... *with* the dancers. The man I had talked with on the phone had gotten only one word wrong. He should have said, "Dessert with the dancers."

We were in a very tight spot with little room for a gracious exit. We looked at each other, got up, and simply said we had to leave. It was obvious to the group why we were leaving. We really didn't say anything, but they knew. Without having to say anything, we had set a new standard for our leadership style.

After a week, one agent had the courage to ask us why we'd left so early. He already knew, but he wanted to be sure. I told him I was uncomfortable watching topless dancers, and that for me, it would have been a sin to watch them. I told him what Jesus said: If you even look at a woman with lust in your heart, you've already committed adultery. (See Matthew 5:27–28.)

He disagreed, saying something about the dancing being just an artistic cultural event. I believe he knew I was right.

JESUS' EXAMPLE: A FRIEND OF SINNERS

That was the beginning of my seven-year management career. When you are trying to influence people who have different points of view, you will, sooner or later, find yourself in an uncomfortable situation, though hopefully not one like our experience at the Moulin Rouge.

Our goal as *marketplace ministers* is to influence those around us for the kingdom of God. To be most effective doing that, we need to be in places where unbelievers gather. In business circles, it is not uncommon to be in a hotel where the lounge or bar becomes the place to gather after a meeting.

At times the Lord directs me to go to these places when my business associates are going there. I know that some may disagree with my actions. But when the workday is finished is usually the time people open up about their lives. It's the best time to get to know them.

I typically order a Coca-Cola so that people can see I'm not drinking alcohol. I never, however, say anything about someone else's choice to drink alcohol. I'm interested in the condition of their spiritual heart, not the issues of the flesh.

There are times when the Holy Spirit prompts me to leave early from these gatherings. I consider that being led of God's Spirit is the key component in my attempts to be with unbelievers under these kinds of circumstances.

The goal is reaching the lost or misguided. Jesus is the perfect role model for this. He was among the people where they lived. He didn't expect them to come to Him; He went to them. He was among sinners and was considered by them as their friend. (See Matthew 11:19.) Yet He remained sinless. He wants us to do the same.

I continued to work toward future promotions in management, but I still didn't have my priorities in the proper order. It was as if I were seeing through a fog. Sometimes I could see clearly what I should do; sometimes I didn't have the slightest idea how far off course I was.

As I mentioned before, ministry was not above work in my priorities. I don't mean to imply that you should tell everyone around you about Jesus every day and that you shouldn't be concerned about getting your work done.

In fact, if that sounds like you, you would be in trouble if you were my employee. We would first have a long talk about why you were sharing Jesus but not getting your work done. If our talk didn't work, then, as one Christian to another, I would fire you. It would be the best lesson I could teach you.

Your work is part of your Christian testimony and ministry to the Lord. The apostle Paul writes in Colossians 3:22–23 that slaves must obey their masters, and they must do their work as if they are doing it for the Lord. If Paul can tell *slaves* to do their work as unto God, then surely employees must be expected to do the same.

I'm not saying that if the Holy Spirit prompts you to do something that you shouldn't do it. When He says to do something, we should do it when He tells us to. Sometimes it will not be convenient or comfortable for you, and sometimes it could negatively affect your occupation in some way, but you must obey. The Lord knows what He is doing.

One time my wife and I were at a dinner with one of the leaders of the company I work for now. He and his wife were sitting right next to us. His wife leaned over to Maralee and said, "I think there are many roads to heaven. What do you think?"

There we were, on the spot in the same way as I had been during my initial job interview. And as graciously as my wife could, she disagreed.

The conversation was charged with the spiritual conflict that was going on behind the veil of the spiritual realm we could not see. The question revealed that life-or-death decisions were being weighed out in this woman's heart. We had to be bold. I did not tap my wife on the knee to stop the conversation. It was a time to speak, not to be quiet.

Unfortunately, throughout the earlier years of my career, I missed many opportunities to influence those around me with the gospel. Many times I could sense the Holy Spirit gently nudging me to say something, and I would let it pass. Missed opportunities were simply a reflection of where my priorities were at that time.

Chapter Three

CALLING TO MINISTRY

*B*ecause my priorities were not perfectly aligned with what God intended, I missed many opportunities to influence others with the gospel. More importantly, I even allowed work to become more important than my wife or children at times.

As time passed, I could feel the distance growing between my wife and me. Each step up the corporate ladder continued to require more time and energy. It seemed right for a while, and yet I had less time for my family and less freedom to share the gospel.

Every few years I would ask the Lord whether or not this was the right path for me. Over time, my prayers about this area of my life became more regular and fervent. I could see the path I was on, and I no longer liked it.

It was as if I were climbing a mountain, planning the route to the top. I took each step confidently. I could see the top, and it was just a matter of time before I would get there.

The only problem was that, as I got higher up this mountain, I could see another mountain in the background more clearly, and that was the mountain I was supposed to be climbing.

I was striving to obtain the wrong mountaintop

experience. The mountain I was climbing would never get me to the top of the other mountain. I would have to go back down the mountain and through a valley to get to the right mountain. That's basically what happened to me personally and professionally.

BIRTH OF A MARRIAGE MINISTRY

The last promotion I achieved was a lower-level executive position. The company had just reorganized and flattened the organizational structure a level or two. The position I held no longer existed. I had to change.

Approximately 20 percent of the people in my position were moved out of management, mostly through retirement or by being sent back to sales positions running agencies. Forty percent of the managers were demoted. The other 40 percent were promoted into positions with more responsibility. I was one of the individuals promoted.

It didn't take many months for me to know I wasn't going to like this new position. My basic temperament thrives on independence, and this position had very little of that. My schedule was regularly subject to change by someone above me, so planning my personal life became more difficult. My wife and children were getting less and less attention—and that had to change.

When you don't pay attention to your marriage relationship, you're heading for disaster. I thank God that He got my attention about the perilous place our marriage was in. Maralee kept encouraging me that we should take a fourteen-week course called *Married for Life*, but I felt I didn't have the time. Besides, "Our marriage is better than average," I would say.

Really, that's a dangerous place to be. If 50 percent of marriages end in divorce, average isn't very good or very safe.

I finally agreed to attend the course. It was being offered over a weekend in January in Winnipeg, Canada. It was bitterly cold, something like minus 40 degrees Fahrenheit. If I could get the course done in a weekend, then I considered that Winnipeg in January would be OK.

What I didn't realize was that the course from *Marriage Ministries International* (MMI) couldn't be done in a weekend. The course is once a week for fourteen weeks. That weekend was a training weekend for couples who wanted to help other married couples by leading the course.

MMI is a worldwide ministry that gives married couples tools with which to help their own marriages so they can more effectively fulfill their call to reach the world with the gospel. Often, difficulties in our marriage can get us side-tracked from God's purpose for our lives. MMI's mission is to equip couples to be a model of a godly home in their communities. These homes become lighthouses in their neighborhoods, a place where neighbors will find the Good News of the gospel of Jesus Christ.

We received all fourteen weeks of material in one weekend. It was like putting your mouth on a fire hose and turning the water on. What a rush!

In one short weekend God shook Maralee and me to the core of our marriage. I discovered that the only way I should gauge how I was doing as a husband was by comparing myself with how Christ treats the church (His bride). Paul tells us in Ephesians 5:25 that, as husbands, we are to love our wives "as Christ also loved the church and gave Himself up for her."

God was saying that an average marriage was no longer good enough. He was challenging me to do my part in having an *excellent* marriage. It's funny how a man can strive to be excellent in sports, business—just about anything but his marriage. The typical man even does well at courting his future bride. But some time after he says, "I do," average becomes good enough. It's not!

Something broke in me that weekend. The Lord was speaking to me profoundly, and I was listening. Part of me had been resisting His best plans for my life, and I had barely felt it before this time.

My marriage had been a reflection of how I related to the Lord. I wasn't completely open with Maralee. I had secrets deep in me that I didn't want her to know about. I was ashamed to admit that I secretly looked at pornography at times when I traveled away from home. Hotels often provided pornographic images that I chose to watch.

I decided to tell Maralee. The apostle James wrote that we need to confess our sins to one another and pray for one another that we may be healed. (See James 5:16.) Besides confessing our sins to God, we must confess to the person we've wronged. Even though

Maralee didn't know what I was doing, deep within her spirit, she sensed that something wasn't right.

I tried to tell myself that these images where harmless and didn't affect anyone but me, but I knew better. Any sexual activity outside the marriage covenant affects the intimacy of the marriage, whether it occurs before or during the marriage.

I was an imperfect man, and that was hard to admit, let alone talk to my wife about. My life wasn't completely given to her, and the same could be said for my relationship with the Lord. I was building my kingdom first, and then His will be done. Not anymore!

I prayed: "Lord, You are first. I don't want to hold anything back. Maralee is second, and our children right after her. Lord, then I must place what You would have me do [ministry] before the work I do."

Afterward, my heart was full of renewed desire to serve the Lord with all my might. Deep inside I sensed a new breakthrough in my spiritual life that was triggered by the new level of transparency I was willing to have with my wife.

The apostle Peter writes in 1 Peter 3:7 that husbands need to live with their wives in an understanding way, otherwise their prayers will be hindered. I began to see how important it was to have a right relationship with my wife and that if the relationship with her wasn't right, it would affect my intimacy with my heavenly Father.

A New Work Begins

With the breakthrough in our marriage that cold

January weekend in Winnipeg, I felt the Lord drawing me into a calling for the five-fold ministry of Ephesians 4:11–12. It was a calling that Maralee had sensed was upon me much earlier, and she had often asked me if I was sure I shouldn't be in the ministry. I didn't know how yet, but I began to explore the possibilities in my heart and mind about whether or not this was from the Lord.

I shared with Maralee that I thought the Lord wanted me to pastor. I didn't know how or when, but that's the call that resonated within me. Responding to this call would mean change; it was an awesomely terrifying thought. At this point, I simply knew what the Lord wanted me to say: *Yes, Lord. Anything. I want Your will for my life.*

As the weekend came to a close, the leadership couples prayed over us and released us. One of the leaders, Jan Taylor, could sense that God was doing a work in me. She encouraged me to respond to what God was putting in me by sharing it with the group.

I shared with the group about the pastoral anointing that I felt God was imparting to me. I didn't know how it all fit yet. I was simply responding to what the Lord gave me to do. It was part of the mantle God placed on me then.

I can't tell you how many times since then that people in and out of the church ask me if I am a pastor. I don't pastor a local church, but I do respond to many people through a pastoral giftedness.

That weekend in January 1996 was the beginning of a decision by Maralee and me to change the course of our lives. We came back from Winnipeg with more questions than answers.

We knew God had begun a new work in us and that He was preparing us for something new. We knew that we would become involved in MMI to help other marriages while we were working on our own. Still, we didn't know how everything would fit together. It was an unsettling time.

The next six months were a time of great upheaval. Our marriage was shaken and sifted through and found to be in need of many modifications. The direction I was going in my career felt more and more wrong, but the salary and benefits, let alone the prestige, were hard to consider giving up. The light breezes of change were turning into winds of hurricane strength. It was inevitable that change would come.

We made plans to lead a *Married for Life* course in our home with six other couples. That was our first step in obeying God's leading.

We knew that at the very least God wanted us involved in ministry to couples so that our own marriage would be strengthened. By sowing marriage principles into others, we reaped those principles as fruit in our own marriage.

We knew that if our own marriage wasn't strong, the enemy could easily get us off track from our calling. He would simply bring division between us to get us off focus.

UNCERTAINTY AND A BREAKTHROUGH

Work was next. Around May 1996, the Lord began to speak to me about stepping off the corporate ladder of success.

One day while I was traveling home from a business meeting, I felt led to take a different route home. I traveled through a small city named Brainerd. I wondered if any agent for the company I worked for might be retiring soon. Maybe I could step down from my executive position and take over an insurance agency again.

The thought wouldn't leave me. The next day I phoned a friend whose management territory included Brainerd. I asked if any of the three agents in that area were considering retirement. My question caught him off guard, but he knew why I was asking.

Sure enough, one of the agents had just quietly mentioned that he was considering early retirement. It appeared that God was at work in this situation. I was excited about the possibilities and couldn't wait to share it with Maralee.

When I first mentioned it to her, she was excited, but this would change before we finally got God's will on the matter. Being the master salesman I am, I began to sell Maralee on the idea of moving—and that was a mistake.

The Lord was challenging me to move in agreement with my wife. My trying to convince her that it was God's plan was not agreement. Agreement, God's way, is for two believers to seek Him individually for His will. When both are confident they have heard from Him and have the same answer, that couple can be assured they have God's answer in the matter.

God does call the husband to be the leader of the home, but that doesn't mean the man should minimize the fact that God also speaks to his wife. God's way of agreement eliminates the potential for future strife after the decision has been made.

Because I tried to sell Maralee on the idea of moving, her walls came up, and that made it hard for both of us to hear from the Lord. We prayed more fervently over this matter than we had previously over any other decision in our marriage. Moving meant leaving friends and a local church that we loved being a part of. Moving meant finding a new house. Most of all, moving meant a change of direction for our lives.

For months we had no clear answer. We were at a crossroads and didn't know what to do. *If we left the security of an executive leadership position, why not leave the company altogether and pastor a local church?* we asked. The nest we had built in life was becoming very unsettled.

At about that time we planned to vacation at Strawberry Lake Christian Retreat in Detroit Lakes, Minnesota.

Founded by Gerald and Beulah Derstine, the retreat is a wonderful Spirit-filled center where families can go to be refreshed and hear from God for direction in their lives.

Billy Joe Daugherty was going to be the guest speaker that week at the retreat center. When I was a student at Oral Roberts University, I had attended Daugherty's church, Victory Christian Center. I was very impressed with his influence and humility as a leader in the body of Christ. Now, fourteen years later, in 1996, God was about to use him to deliver a pivotal message at a crossroads in my life.

Up to that point in 1996, my life had been consumed with work; my focus had become more and more about me and less about God's kingdom. I was on a "train" going someplace I didn't want to go, and I didn't know how to get off. I was thirty-five years old and counting the years left to an early retirement at fifty-five. *Then I would serve the Lord more fully,* I thought.

The reality of that train ride was that, at age fifty-five, some other cares of this world would come along and draw me away from serving Jesus Christ first. Most of my dreams had really been about me, about what I could accumulate for myself. I did want to do things for the Lord, but only if they fit into my plans and schedule, and they usually didn't.

I had become frustrated with the tension, and neither Maralee nor I knew what to do. Praise God, the breakthrough was finally coming.

Billy Joe delivered a powerful message about serving God first. He shared a vision God had given him about people who were focused only on themselves. They were marching in a line, one after another, directly to the edge of a cliff. They didn't know what they were doing until it was too late. They fell off the cliff into hell before they could do anything about it.

He passionately challenged us to embrace the fact that the Christian life is more than having a job and eventually retiring with a place on the lake and a boat by the dock. He said our purpose in life is to reach the lost. It is about serving Christ first. It is about answering God's call to be His minister.

My heart was beating wildly. God was speaking to me. *What kind of life was I going to choose?* God was calling my name. Like Abraham of the Bible, God was simply asking me to follow Him. I didn't know where I was going, only that I needed to go. Again, I said yes to the Lord's call.

This was the second time in about six months that I could sense the strong calling of God that would require change. In that moment, my life changed. His kingdom was now first. I wasn't just saying it. It was first in my actions. I wanted His heart in every matter, not just for my benefit, but also for the benefit of those around me.

"Not my will, but Your will be done through me, Father God," was my prayer. It was a divine, holy moment. I knew a breakthrough had taken place inside me, yet I still did not know the direction for our lives.

We talked to Billy Joe about our passion to help married couples. We even talked about moving to Tulsa and working with married couples in his church. Although it would have been exciting being in Tulsa again, we sensed God had something different in mind.

We also talked with Pastor Phil Derstine from Florida about assisting him, but again we felt God had something different for us. God had definitely called me into the ministry, but He had something I didn't expect. He was calling me to be a *marketplace minister*. It hadn't really dawned on me yet, but that was what was coming forth.

Issues of lust and pride in my heart had been exposed and dealt with. My marriage was being transformed. Maralee and I could see that the Lord had a plan for ministry that we would be doing together. Now the Lord was sending me forth with a new level of Spirit-filled power and authority that I had not experienced before. A new work was beginning.

A DOOR OPENS IN BRAINERD

God made it clear to both of us that He wanted us to move to Brainerd and take over the insurance agency. Maralee and I were in agreement before the Lord. The new position would become more than just provision for us; it would become a position of influence for the kingdom of God. God also spoke to us about helping to plant the ministry of MMI (now called University of the Family) across Minnesota.

We became the state leaders for the ministry. Over the next few years, we wrestled with understanding our role in the marketplace, wanting to know for sure that we had heard the Lord's leading. Even so, we sensed that God was pleased with our decision. Our role in MMI had been to develop leaders across Minnesota who lead *Married for Life* seminars in home Bible studies and to develop leadership couples who help us oversee areas of the state for MMI.

We moved to Brainerd, and we sensed our ministry with MMI was going to be a big part of what God was asking us to do. But, as I mentioned earlier, I was still unsure of God's plan for me as an insurance agent. We were doing what we believed we should with the ministry calling, but I was floundering at work. I was having trouble with the transition back to an agency. It didn't feel right, or at least I didn't seem to be approaching it right.

Really, the only thing that was going well was our ministry assignment. We answered God's call by saying, "Yes, Lord—anything," and we found ourselves rowing our boat into unknown waters with a storm blowing all around us. We left our home, church and friends and moved to an unfamiliar place.

We bought another large family-sized house on a lake, thinking our other lake home would sell right away. It didn't. We owned two houses for about a year and a half, and I was making less than half of the salary to which we were accustomed. I was no longer climbing a corporate ladder, and it seemed that what I was doing in the marketplace was less significant. We were in an emotional storm.

One Wednesday evening, while attending our new church, we responded to an altar call for prayer. Pastor Russell Kalenberg prayed prophetically over us that we were in a *megastorm*, but God was bringing us *megapeace*.

At that moment, though we still were in a storm, His peace poured over us and settled within us. Despite our storm, God was confirming His path for us with signs and wonders. We asked the Lord to bring forth leaders for MMI in the Brainerd area.

Actually, He had begun to do just that the first time I visited the church in Brainerd, before we moved there. I was in the third row during a Sunday morning service. Pastor Kalenberg encouraged us to greet one another during one part of the service, and the couple in front of me—Randy and Gayle Cousins—turned around to say hello.

They asked if I was visiting the area, and I said that my family and I were planning to move to the area. They asked what we would be doing in the area. Normally I would have said I was going to run an insurance agency in the area, but on this occasion I said we were moving to Brainerd to plant a ministry for married couples.

Right away I saw the excitement God was building in their hearts for this kind of ministry. They had been married for about twenty years. At their wedding ceremony, the pastor had prophesied that the Lord would use them to help other married couples. This was now coming to pass. They ended up being our first assistants in the Brainerd area.

In addition, a few weeks after we moved to the area, we attended our children's Christmas program at their school. It was an opportunity for our children to meet some of their new classmates, and for us to meet some of the other parents.

One father, Dwane Menke, was chasing his energetic son all around the social hall. Maralee had said to me, "I think you should go meet that guy." Well, I really wasn't in the social mood, so I didn't respond to her request. She persisted, and I continued to resist. Finally, after she decided to leave it alone, I suddenly had the great idea that I *should* go meet that guy chasing his son around.

Dwane and his wife, Denise, had lived in the area for only six months. We chatted for a bit, and I asked Dwane if he had ever heard of MMI. Strangely enough, they had just signed up to be in an MMI group before they moved to Brainerd.

After a while, I finally came to the realization that all coincidences are really "God-incidences." He was divinely drawing leaders to us and confirming our path with signs and wonders.

God 'Speaks' at Gilbert Lake

Probably the most unique God-incidence to date is how the Lord connected us with Pastors Flo and Mary Kubes. Flo and Mary live in the small city of Faribault, about four hours south of Brainerd. We had received their names from a mutual friend who thought they might be interested in MMI.

I phoned Flo to see if he might be interested in having MMI in his church and community. He graciously said that he wasn't interested. While we visited over the phone, he shared that his family was going to be on vacation in the Brainerd area and that they were going to stay at the Gilbert Lake Resort.

I thought that uniquely coincidental because our house is on the same lake. We live in a county that has four hundred lakes and hundreds of resort locations, but Flo and Mary had picked Gilbert Lake Resort. Flo ended the conversation by saying that perhaps when they were in Brainerd they would get together with us.

Now, if you know anything about pastors, you know that their family vacations are very important. By the time Flo and Mary had gotten to the resort, they had no plans of seeing us, and they never told tell us when they were coming.

One day during their vacation, they took out one of the resort pontoon boats for a cruise on the water. After they got out into the lake, their motor quit working. They couldn't paddle back to the resort; the wind was strongly blowing them in the opposite direction across the lake.

Flo tried vigorously time and time again to start the motor by pulling the ignition cord, but eventually he resigned himself to the fact that they were going to blow onto someone's beach, and they would have to ask for help.

God is amazing! They were blown onto *our* beach. Flo sheepishly came up to the house and asked Maralee if he could borrow the phone to ask the resort management for help. He asked Maralee exactly where he was so he could give the resort directions.

"You're at the Gazelkas," she said.

Maralee said his mouth dropped open. He decided right then that they needed to get together with us to talk about MMI. I surmised that if he didn't respond then, the Lord might have had to use a whale to convince him! And by the way—after Flo's call to the resort, he went back to the pontoon, and with one pull of the ignition cord, the motor started, and off they went!

God was confirming His ministry calling to Maralee and me in many ways, but I needed to feel comfortable that the marketplace was still where He wanted us as well. It took me a long time to get to where God was leading me, but He was patient. He was bringing it forth.

Chapter Four

THE CALL TO
THE MARKETPLACE
REAFFIRMED

*S*tepping off the corporate ladder was a decision that initially would cut our income by more than half, but God calls many ministers to earn all of their provision from preaching the gospel. I was tentative at first, but over the next few years, I settled back into the marketplace as an insurance agent. I began to see the incredible influence I could have for the kingdom of God through my marketplace work.

My insurance agency has almost two thousand families as clients. That means that whenever a significant event occurs in the life of someone I insure, they usually come to my office to tell me about it.

We don't just sell them insurance; we help them through difficult situations and celebrate with them during joyful occasions. In my agency I often function as a pastor would. As the Spirit of God leads, I minister Christ, mostly through actions, and sometimes through words.

One day a client came into the office. He was rather gloomy. He wanted to remove his wife as beneficiary from his life-insurance policy. It didn't take the Spirit of God to tell me something was wrong; it was obvious.

I probed and asked why he was removing his wife

from the policy. He said they were divorcing. He was broken up inside, and it was difficult for him not to show it.

My heart went out to him, and I shared that even in this difficult situation, God would help him through. I then asked if he had a personal relationship with Jesus, and he said he did not. Right there in the office, we came before the throne of God together, and he received Jesus Christ as Savior.

After we had finished praying, he said that just a few days before he had opened a Bible for the first time in decades, trying to find some answers to his problems. He was knocking, and the Lord answered his heart's cry through my obedience.

EXCELLENCE AND INFLUENCE IN WORK AND MINISTRY

Leading people to Christ in my office is not a common event. It happens maybe once or twice a year. More often my staff and I listen, and sometimes pray with people going through personal calamities.

One time on the way home from ministering in another city, Maralee and I came upon a severe traffic accident. There was a great ball of fire burning in the middle of the road. A drunken driver, traveling at speeds near one hundred miles per hour, had hit another vehicle head-on. The drunken driver and the two people in the other car all were dead.

We were on the scene well before the police arrived. Two cars had arrived just before us, and the drivers were looking in the ditch for any survivors. There were none. I chose not to go into the ditch when

I was told how gruesome the scene was. My wife and I simply stayed at the scene for about thirty minutes, praying in the Spirit for the families that were going to be deeply affected by this terrible tragedy.

I didn't realize at the time that one of the victims killed by the drunk driver was a client of mine—a sixteen-year-old girl, who had died with her boyfriend. I had visited with her just a few months earlier about the privileges of driving. Her life was unnecessarily snuffed out.

I can't tell you how much it meant to her family to know that I was at the scene of the tragedy and that I had already begun to pray for the families involved. We wept together in my office. God used me to help them through their time of sorrow.

Ministry in the marketplace was no longer difficult for me. The difficulty became doing my chosen profession with excellence.

I knew now without a shadow of doubt that I was called as a minister, but I wasn't exactly sure how to function as a professional insurance agent. I wanted to do it with excellence, but what was excellent? In my heart, work had swung on a pendulum from too important to unimportant. I knew the two, work and ministry, were not yet in proper balance.

The Lord wants our lives to be influential for the kingdom of God. So the question is, *Where can I be most influential?*

If the marketplace is part of that calling, and if we do our work with excellence, will it bring more influence? The answer is emphatically, *yes!* Excellence brings influence. Proverbs 18:16 reminds us that our gift brings us before great people.

That happened to me a few years ago when the insurance company I work for built a new regional office. Minnesota's lieutenant governor was on hand for the ribbon-cutting ceremony, as well as many other state dignitaries. I was asked to perform the invocation.

I was honored for having the privilege of asking the Lord for His blessing and direction for this event. Why did they choose me? It wasn't because I was acknowledged as a devout Christian man; others in the organization were as well. It was because I was acknowledged as a person of excellence within the organization who also was a devout Christian. Excellence brings influence.

I knew that if I couldn't continue to do my job with excellence, I shouldn't do it at all. Could I be excellent in the marketplace as well as in ministry? That's what I was still trying to figure out.

THE CALLING CONFIRMED

Over the years I have developed a friendship with evangelist and motivational speaker Mark Gorman. He was on a similar journey of being called to the marketplace and to ministry, but from the other direction. He was a minister first, yet he felt called to pursue marketplace activities as well.

At that point in our friendship, though, it wasn't clear that marketplace and ministry could mix. I sent him an e-mail that expressed the heartfelt desire I had to serve the Lord in the marketplace, but also as a minister. Mark responded back saying he wasn't sure if that would fit for me.

Then, for the first time, I put to paper (literally to e-mail) what I believed the Lord had been speaking to me. I wrote back to Mark and said that I believed I was called to both the five-fold ministry and the marketplace. I was making a declaration that was breaking down walls in my mind and in the spirit about this dual calling. I believed I could do both. I had to do both!

Mark was quick to respond by saying that a dual calling was possible. In fact, throughout my spiritual journey he has been one of my greatest supporters and encouragers.

The next day my wife and I traveled to Duluth, Minnesota, to attend a special church service at the Glad Tidings Assembly of God. Harold Eatmon was the guest speaker. At the time, I had never met Harold, but I had heard that he moved strongly in a prophetic gift. I really didn't want to go at first, but Maralee had a strong desire to be there.

We prayed about it together and decided we would go. I had an expectation that the Lord was going to speak to me through Harold.

As he ministered, it was apparent that the prophetic gift within him was very accurate and had matured over a long period of time. At one point in the service he asked if he could pray for me, and I responded affirmatively. The Lord showed Harold where I had been, and where I was going.

However, the most profound thing Harold said was: "You have been called to be a leader in the five-fold ministry, and you have been called to be a leader in the marketplace."

He knew nothing about me in a natural sense. He didn't know I was in business and passionate about ministry. He didn't know I had just sent Mark Gorman an e-mail with that very declaration.

The timing was of the Lord. Harold's words hit me deep within my spirit, confirming the path the Lord was laying before me. For the first time I felt I could run passionately with the dual vision of ministry and marketplace that God had given me for my life.

Until then, I had felt I didn't belong, and I was uncomfortable in both roles. When I was at a business function among peers, I longed to be ministering. When I was among a group of pastors, I felt I didn't fit in as a peer, that I was just a layman.

Now I didn't care what others thought. I knew both ministry and marketplace were part of one plan God had for me.

Since that meeting at Glad Tidings Assembly, God has confirmed the same message to me through three other Christian leaders, two of whom had not met me when they prophetically declared the same word to me as Harold Eatmon had. The Lord knew I needed to "know that I know that I know" that this was His plan for me. He spoke it in my heart, and confirmed it in my ministry and work, and then He declared it to me prophetically through some of his servants.

The walls of limitation that I set for myself—and that

some other people helped to build—about what my role should be and what I should be doing are gone. I'm free to think more strategically about how God may want to use me to further His kingdom. I see part of my role as connecting Christian leaders from the marketplace and professional ministry to increase their effectiveness in their spheres of authority.

Opportunities for Ministry

A few years ago, I had the opportunity to be a chaplain at a large secular country-music festival in Detroit Lakes, Minnesota. The event was a mixture of alcohol and music, producing a wild atmosphere for fifty thousand raving fans.

As chaplains, we were assigned the responsibility of walking the camp grounds to see if we could help the attendees in any way. Believe me, some of them needed a lot of help. Invariably the opportunity to share Christ came up.

Pastor Phil Derstine of Florida and I walked together and discussed how we could do this same type of witnessing at car-racing events. Brainerd is a strategic site for National Hot Rod Association (NHRA) racing—drag racing. One event alone draws more than one hundred thousand fans during four days of racing.

The Lord put it on my heart to approach Sheriff Dick Ross, who is also a believer, about having chaplains at the raceway. Together we agreed this should be done.

The idea was birthed, and now the chaplains at

the raceway are under the authority of the local police chaplain. Volunteer chaplains, consisting of pastors and other mature Christians from the marketplace, come from our community. Our presence is making a positive impact at the raceway in the same way it did at the country-music festival. There is less serious mischief, and many people are influenced by the gospel.

Once, as some of us were walking the raceway grounds, I came upon a woman who was getting demonstrably drunk. A man, who was also thoroughly intoxicated, was making moves on her that she wasn't resisting very effectively. I could tell what his motive was, and she didn't seem to care about it.

She saw the large crosses on our T-shirts and yelled out that she was a Christian, too. It turned out that she had recently divorced her husband and was trying to drown the pain in alcohol. We had the opportunity to express the love of Christ to her and remind her how much Christ cared for her.

As we talked, she mentioned that she went to a church in Minneapolis called Living Word. I told her that I recently had spent some time with her pastor. Suddenly, conviction came upon her when she realized I knew her pastor. Obviously she knew that he wouldn't approve of where she was. More importantly, God knew where she was spiritually, and that she was in a dangerous place.

We had the opportunity to pray for reconciliation in her marriage and that the Lord would bless her. When we finished, she went back to her camper, leaving the guy who had been hounding her. The Lord used us to intervene in her life.

MARKETPLACE MINISTERS: PART OF GOD'S END-TIME STRATEGY

Over the last few years, I've thought more about defining who I am because I've discovered that there are many Christians like me, called to both five-fold ministry and the marketplace. It's been accepted that a believer in the marketplace should provide financial resources to the local church, supporting the local pastor's vision and contributing to other ministries as well. It's also encouraged that a believer should evangelize within his or her individual sphere of influence, inviting friends, neighbors and co-workers to church.

I agree that all of that is important. I also believe there is much more potential for the marketplace minister.

Marketplace ministers have a part in the End-Time strategy for reaching the world with the gospel. All kingdom strategy comes from God, and He decides who is best equipped and ready to bring it forth. Sometimes it is a local pastor or group of pastors working together. Sometimes it's someone in the marketplace.

I believe that, in the future, we will see much of the strategy coming from pastors and marketplace leaders working together as peers to bring forth God's plan for a city, state, nation and for the world. Someone invariably is called to lead. Sometimes it will be a pastor-turned-apostle; sometimes it will be a marketplace minister functioning as an apostle, but the Lord must decide, not us. I use the word *apostle* because Ephesians 2:20 says apostles and prophets build the foundation.

The thought that marketplace ministers are on an equal plane with professional ministers has resonated in me for a long time, but I didn't know how to articulate it without sounding like a heretic. Understanding authority and how to flow *under* it first so that you can flow *in* it is the critical principle here. (I will talk more about this in chapter eight.)

The last thing I wanted to do was get off track with what God wanted me to do. I didn't want pride or deception to lead me out of God's plan for my life. I was looking for confirmation that the Spirit of God was speaking to me and that what was being revealed to me was from the Lord.

The Lord put it on my heart to visit with John Kelly. John functions as an apostle. I met him through another ministry board on which we both serve. I immediately liked John and was drawn to the spiritual gifts within him. Being around him had the tendency to pull me to higher levels in Christ, and I needed that.

He asked me if I wanted to travel with him to Mexico, where he was going to be part of a large crusade in December 2001. From the start I was excited about the opportunity, but when I looked at my schedule, I wasn't sure if I could fit it in. I didn't pray seriously about it; I just set it aside.

The Holy Spirit prompted Maralee three times to ask me if I was sure I shouldn't be going. That alone ought to have been enough for me to get quiet before God and see what He had to say about it. Maralee loves going south in mid-winter, but she was willing to stay in frozen Minnesota and send me down to warm Mexico in December. That also should have been a clue to me to seek God.

At the last moment, less than a week before the event, I realized how important going to Mexico with John was for me. I booked the ticket, at a much higher rate than I would have gotten had I done it earlier, but it didn't matter—I needed to be obedient.

During my preparations to go, I wrote down some of my thoughts about my role as a Christian leader. I was trying to put into words a way to describe my calling in ministry and my calling in the marketplace. It was the first time I thought about describing myself as a marketplace minister.

I wrote it down, "marketplace minister." It was the best way for me to describe that I felt every bit a minister and that I still had provision and influence in the marketplace. After writing down what I wanted to share with John, I settled in for a long series of flights that would eventually take me to Rocco Blanca Mission Base in southern Mexico.

During the flights I began to read a book titled *God @ Work* by Rich Marshall. The book had been given to me a few weeks earlier by a businessman who had heard me share about work and ministry. The timing of reading the book was confirmation to me that I was on the right path.

The book talked about ministers in the market-place, exactly what I had just called myself. It also mentioned a couple in Minneapolis, Dennis and Megan Doyle, who were very involved in ministry and very successful in business. I decided that when I got back to Minnesota I would call the Doyles and visit. I finished the book during the last flight, encouraged by it and further excited to visit with John in Mexico.

A missionary named Brad Clere was waiting at the airport. We talked a bit, and I discovered that of the two churches supporting him, one was a congregation my wife and I attended when we lived in western Minnesota. The other was a small church in Chouteau, Oklahoma, that I had also visited. Brad and I discovered we had a mutual friend in the ministry.

The world is large, but the Lord sure makes us feel right at home wherever He leads us. Meeting up with Brad was more confirmation that He was divinely orchestrating my itinerary.

Spending time with John was strategic for my life's course. Our week together developed our relation-ship into a spiritual father-and-son connection. He confirmed that what was in my heart was of God and was happening around the world.

Then he said he wanted me to meet some people in Minneapolis when I got to Minnesota—Dennis and Megan Doyle! Only two days before, I had seen their names while reading on my flight to Mexico and had decided to get in contact with them. Now John was telling me to meet them. Everything was falling into place, and God was confirming it with signs and wonders.

I humbly submit to you that I am a marketplace minister. I believe that my role is to influence the world through my marketplace position. I'm also called to equip the saints in a variety of positions of authority. God gives me strategies to reach my city, state and nation, as well as the world. I have a part to play, and I'm running the race set before me.

What about you? Are you a marketplace minister? Are you called into the five-fold ministry but also called into the marketplace? God will confirm His plan for you, too.

PART TWO: IMPARTATION

Chapter Five

THE GREAT PARADIGM SHIFT

*T*his is what I call the "rubber meets the road" chapter. After you see yourself as a minister, no matter what you are doing, you will be thinking about how to further the kingdom of God. Marketplace ministers need to understand who they are in order to be effective in their calling. There are some obstacles to becoming settled in this calling, so let's talk about them plainly.

First, here's my definition of a marketplace minister: *Marketplace ministers* are men and women God has called into the ministry and who retain ties to the marketplace and draw their primary income from it.

They are ministers of the gospel. Their marketplace ties create influence for the kingdom of God and provide provision for kingdom works. The provision is to help fulfill the vision that God has given to other men and women in the ministry, but just as important, the provision is to help fulfill the vision within the marketplace minister.

This connection between ministry and marketplace is not "unfortunate"; it is not "less than the perfect will of God"; it is what God originally intended when He set the church in motion. It's more than inviting the "sinners" to church. It's bringing church to them.

The kingdom of God is within us. It's not just quoting the Bible to lost souls; it is also presenting the living Word to them through our daily lives. If we are to reach the lost at any cost, then we must go where they are! We must go to the "highways and byways" and compel them to come in to the wedding feast, the kingdom of God. (See Matthew 22:1–10.) We must be "in" the world but not "of" it.

Now let's look at some of the mindsets that get in the way of flowing in this calling.

Misconceptions are like roadblocks—without removing them you can't go forward on your journey. So, let's clear up some roadblocks. By focusing on the truth, misconceptions become more obvious.

Have you ever noticed when you make a cash deposit in a bank how quickly the teller flips through the money? It's amazing how quickly they can count it.

Bank tellers are "called" to handle money. In addition to counting it quickly, they are also trained to spot counterfeit money. If you give them a stack of fifty-dollar bills, because they are trained properly, they can immediately recognize a counterfeit bill. They are trained to recognize the counterfeit by first studying the real thing.

The only time they have difficulty distinguishing real from counterfeit is when a new design is created for a bill. Then it takes some adjustment time to become comfortable with what the new one looks like.

The concept of marketplace ministers is not new, but it feels like a newly created design for ministry. Like the new fifty-dollar bill, it will take some time for the church to adjust and be comfortable with this kind of minister, but by studying what a real minister looks like, we can see that marketplace ministers are truly full-fledged ministers of the gospel.

Let's look at four principles that can be applied to ministers, and then focus specifically on application to marketplace ministers.

MARKETPLACE MINISTERS ARE FULL-TIME MINISTERS

You might be questioning me right now about how that can be if the person isn't receiving all their wages from preaching the gospel. If how we receive wages is the only criterion for what we consider full-time ministry, you are correct. If that is so, then I would like to change the definition of full-time ministry.

I believe we all are called to be full-time ministers for the kingdom of God. In Mark 16:15 we are all told by Jesus to go into all the world and preach the gospel. It was a commission for all those who are disciples of Jesus. In 2 Corinthians 5:18–20, the apostle Paul identifies us all as ministers of reconciliation. He goes on to say we are all ambassadors for Christ.

This isn't a 9 A.M. to 5 P.M. calling; it is 24/7—twenty four hours a day, seven days a week. We all are called full time, all the time. It's simply a matter of how we uniquely express the callings that differ among us.

I think we all would agree that a pastor of a local church is considered part of the full-time ministry. In a typical pastor's week, you will see him prepare and deliver two or three sermons. He will likely have had meetings and counseling sessions throughout the week. He will typically have had regular personal devotion time with the Lord. Hopefully he will also have spent time with his wife and family. And throughout the week he will have spent numerous hours with the everyday activities that are common to all of us: paying bills, driving the car, eating, sleeping and so on. It's a full-time position.

If you noticed, many of the same activities a pastor does are activities that we all have in our days. We all spend personal time with the Lord. If we are sensitive to the Spirit, we will often have divine meetings and counseling sessions with people around us. If we are married, when we are at home, we spend time ministering to our spouses and children. And throughout the week we will spend numerous hours on the everyday activities common to all of us, paying bills, driving the car, eating, sleeping and more.

Everyone has the same full-time calling before the Lord. Occupation and salary don't determine the fullness of calling; the Lord does. As I've said already, if we are focused on the Lord's work, we will likely have regular divine appointments with those around us. My heart before God says, "Lord, what do You want to do through me today?" Throughout everyday life, I'm learning to be sensitive to the Holy Spirit's promptings. I'm available 24/7.

One morning in my prayer time I told the Lord that I was available for His plans. As that morning unfolded, I took my car to the dealership for repairs. The dealer agreed to provide a ride for me back to work while my car was being repaired.

I wasn't really thinking about witnessing to the young man who was assigned to drive me back to my office, but it seemed as if I had very little choice. Without my prompting, he poured out his heart to me. He told me how much of a mess his life was. His girlfriend was pregnant, and he didn't want to marry her—and that was just the tip of the iceberg.

After about five minutes of his tirade, I stopped him in his tracks and simply said, "You need Jesus!" It just welled up inside me and came out with conviction. The Lord helped me shift the focus from his problems to the solution—Jesus Christ. Before we got to my office, I had a new brother in Christ.

Our lives must be viewed as full-time ministry. Even temporal things like getting a ride to work can have spiritual significance. We are all full-time ministers, so taking a day off is not an option.

One time when Pastor Phil Derstine and I were walking through the campgrounds as chaplains at "We Fest"—a rowdy country-music festival—we ran into one very inebriated fan with battery-operated devil horns attached to his head. He would proudly push a button, and the horns would light up.

We were wearing T-shirts with big white crosses and the word *Chaplain* on them. It seemed as if our shirts glowed in the dark with the anointing of God on them. They really stood out.

When the horned devil's friends saw that we were ministers, they were quick to get their friend into trouble. To our surprise, they said their devil-faced friend was actually a youth pastor taking a break from his ministry obligations. If he was a believer in Christ, he had forgotten that we are all called to ministry full time.

Phil was much more pastoral than I would have been. He took the time to help this misguided man see his folly by helping him focus on why he wanted to help youth in the first place. God has a sense of humor. I'm sure that youth pastor will never forget how God paged him at "We Fest" to get back on the job.

In the name of equal treatment for pastors, here's a story of a church member who forgot she was called full time to represent Christ. Pastor Mike Bang recently shared a humorous story with me about an incident that happened to him.

He drove to a stop light with one vehicle in front of him. As the light turned green, he noticed the vehicle in front of him had a bumper sticker that read, "Honk if you love Jesus." Mike loves Jesus, so he responded to the bumper sticker with a tap on his horn.

The driver in front of him assumed Mike was honking to get her moving. She responded with the universal hand sign that, nicely interpreted, means "I don't like you or what you are doing." I hope she didn't attend his church.

Marketplace ministers are in the full-time ministry. Everywhere we go we are ambassadors for Christ. God is orchestrating His will all around us, and with sensitivity to His leading, we get to participate in furthering His kingdom.

MINISTRY LEADERS ARE CALLED
TO EQUIP THE SAINTS

Those in leadership are called to help Christians become more effective at functioning together, in order to influence the world with the gospel. These ministers are often said to be part of the five-fold ministry calling. Marketplace ministers also are part of the five-fold ministry calling.

The term *five-fold ministry* comes from Ephesians 4:11–13: "And He gave some as apostles, and some as prophets, and some as evangelists, and some as pastors and teachers, *for the equipping of the saints* for the work of service, to the building up of the body of Christ; until we all attain to the unity of the faith, and of the knowledge of the Son of God, to a mature man, to the measure of the stature which belongs to the fullness of Christ" (emphasis added).

The five leadership positions include apostle, prophet, evangelist, pastor and teacher. At one time I thought these positions were reserved for those individuals who graduated from seminary or left the marketplace and were receiving all of their wages from preaching the gospel. But nowhere in Ephesians 4:11–13 do we see anything about occupation or education.

The key indicator for determining if we are in one of these positions is simply our involvement in equipping the saints for the work of service. The Lord alone is the One who determines who we are and what we will become. As *marketplace ministers*, if we are involved in equipping the saints, either we are part of the five-fold ministry, or we are emerging into the five-fold ministry.

Often we have a sense that God has more for us to do. We see ourselves as something we have not yet become. We have dreams of doing wonderful things for the kingdom of God, but our own maturity level prevents us from accomplishing these dreams. If this is you, don't fret; you are still emerging into your full calling.

As an example, let's look at the apostle Paul. Paul was not always an apostle. After the Lord got his attention on the road to Damascus, he didn't suddenly become an apostle. Paul emerged as an apostle.

In Acts 9 we see the account of Paul, then called Saul, being confronted by Jesus on the road to Damascus. He was wondrously saved, but blinded by his encounter with the Lord.

Then the Lord sent Ananias to find Saul, pray for him to receive his sight and lay hands on him to receive the Holy Spirit. Saul, then filled with the Holy Spirit, immediately began to proclaim that Jesus was the Son of God.

I'm not sure how much revelation Saul had at the time about Jesus, other than the fact that he knew for sure that He was the Son of God and that everyone with whom he came into contact should hear the Good News. His initial proclamations sound a lot like people who get radically saved today. They don't know a whole lot about their salvation, but they sure know they are saved. Just like new believers today,

I'm quite sure Saul was not considered an apostle by any of his contemporaries at that point in his life.

By Acts 13, Paul—still called Saul—had been seeking the Lord diligently for years. In the first verse of Acts 13 we see that Saul was listed among the teachers and prophets of the Antioch church. "Now there were at Antioch, in the church that was there, prophets and teachers: Barnabas, and Simeon who was called Niger, and Lucius of Cyrene, and Manaen who had been brought up with Herod the tetrarch, *and Saul*" (emphasis added).

It is clear from this scripture that Saul was not listed as an apostle yet. He was probably a teacher. In Acts 13:2–3 Saul and Barnabas were set apart by the Holy Spirit for the work He called them to. It is some time after that point that Saul was called by a new name, Paul. Acts 13:9 first mentioned that change of name.

From then on, the Bible documents that Paul and Barnabas were doing the work of apostles. Their apostleship is confirmed in Acts 14:14, where both Paul and Barnabas are described as apostles. Paul *emerged* as an apostle. He wasn't one when he was first saved. Over time, he matured as a believer and for a time was considered a teacher, but not an apostle. He eventually emerged, however, as one of the most influential apostles of all time.

As such, Paul could have asserted his right to receive compensation from the people to whom he ministered. He chose instead to retain a trade, which he used at various times as his provision. Paul was a *marketplace apostle*. In Acts 18:1–3 we discover that he was making tents with Aquila and Priscilla.

> After these things he left Athens and went to
> Corinth. And he found a certain Jew named
> Aquila, a native of Pontus, having recently
> come from Italy with his wife Priscilla,
> because Claudius had commanded all the
> Jews to leave Rome. *He came to them, and
> because he was of the same trade, he stayed with
> them and they were working; for by trade they
> were tent-makers* (emphasis added).

The issue isn't whether or not a minister gets his
provision from preaching the gospel. The issue is
what the Lord has ordained for you to do now, and
what the Lord will ordain for you to do in the future.
The Lord determines our calling. At various times in
his ministry, the apostle Paul chose to work his trade.
At other times he chose not to.

Paul encouraged ministers to receive their wages
from preaching the gospel. He articulated clearly in 1
Corinthians 9:14 that those who proclaim the gospel
should get their living from the gospel, yet curiously
he chose not to. He clarified in 1 Corinthians 9:6 that
both he and Barnabas worked, even though many of
the other apostles did not.

Throughout 1 Corinthians 9 Paul explains that the
reason he doesn't take full advantage of receiving
money from preaching the gospel is for the purpose of
winning even more people to Christ. That is the key:
How can we be most influential for the kingdom of God?

Will a trade give me greater influence for the kingdom of God? Will a trade provide more resources for

me to fulfill my calling?

When my family and I had the opportunity to minister in Peru in February 2002 we ended up paying for our own air fare. Had we not been able to come up with the money for our flight, we would not have been able to go.

The Peruvians are a generous people but do not have the same standard of living that we do in the United States. Four families combined their resources together to furnish an apartment for our family. They all took turns providing for our daily needs.

But some of the churches we attended could not have supported us. At one of the smaller gatherings of about 80 people, they took up an offering for us. It seemed that everyone put something in the bucket at the front of the sanctuary. It added up to what appeared to be a lot of Peruvian money, but when we converted it to U.S. dollars, it amounted to about fifteen dollars.

We were incredibly grateful for their generosity. We felt blessed far beyond any dollar amount of an offering. But if we had exercised our right to receive wages from ministering the gospel, we might not have been able to reach out to as many people as we did.

My trade of insurance created the provision the Lord used to send us. The apostle Paul also did not burden some of the churches he built by requiring financial obligations of them for his work as a minister.

Marketplace ministers can be in leadership positions of the body of Christ. They can be apostle, prophet, evangelist, pastor or teacher. Money or occupation do not determine the leadership calling. God does. In addition, what we are called to do today can develop and change over time, just as it did for the apostle Paul.

MINISTRY AND MARKETPLACE CALLINGS CAN MIX

God does not make us all the same. Neither does He give us all the same combinations of gifts and spheres of influence. The Lord puts ministers of the gospel into all spheres of influence. "Into every person's world," as Oral Roberts says.

We've already established that Paul the apostle worked in the trade of tent-making at various times. Aquila and Priscilla, fellow tent-makers, were also in a leadership position within the body of Christ. We see in 1 Corinthians 16:19 that they were leaders of a church that met in their home.

Their leadership position is further confirmed by how they related to Apollos. Apollos was likely an apostle. Paul placed him on the same ministry level as himself and Peter. In 1 Corinthians 1:12 Paul writes, "Now I mean this, that each one of you is saying, 'I am of Paul,' and 'I of Apollos,' and 'I of Cephas,' and 'I of Christ.' Has Christ been divided?"

Apollos was an apostle, and yet early in his ministry we see Aquila and Priscilla instructing Apollos more clearly in the things of God. Acts 18:24–26 says: "Now a certain Jew named Apollos, an Alexandrian by birth, an eloquent man, came to Ephesus; and he was mighty in the Scriptures. This man had been instructed in the way of the Lord; and being fervent in spirit, he was speaking and teaching accurately the things concerning Jesus, being acquainted only with the baptism of John; and he began to speak out boldly in the synagogue. But when Priscilla and Aquila heard him, they took him aside and explained to him the way of God more accurately."

Only someone in leadership takes another leader aside to explain the things of God more clearly to him. Priscilla and Aquila were marketplace ministers. They made tents for an occupation, but were leaders of the local church that met in their home. They also ministered with Paul.

Luke, the writer of the Books of Luke and Acts, was another *marketplace minister*. We know that he traveled with Paul throughout many of his apostolic journeys, yet Paul still called him the "beloved physician" in Colossians 4:14.

Another *marketplace minister* was Zenas. We don't know much about Zenas, but he was an attorney, and he traveled with Apollos on their apostolic journeys. Paul writes in Titus 3:13: "Diligently help Zenas the lawyer and Apollos on their way so that nothing is lacking for them." Many prominent ministers in the early church had occupations. They were marketplace ministers.

One thing that stands out to me about some of the early marketplace apostles is that they were establishing works among the Gentiles and didn't want to burden them unnecessarily. The Jewish Christians had the established law of the Old Testament as a model for supporting the ministering priests. The Gentile believers didn't have this model, nor did Paul want them to.

Paul encouraged them to be generous financial givers—motivated by love, not law. He wanted them to be free to serve God and others through the law of love.

We can see from Paul's writings in Galatians 2 that he admonished other Jewish believers for piling rules and regulations from the Old Testament law onto the Gentile Christians. This whole issue came to a head, and the apostolic leadership of the entire church gathered to see what the Holy Spirit wanted to do about this dilemma.

The rest of the church leadership ended up agreeing with Paul. James, the earthly brother of Jesus, declared, "Therefore it is my judgment that we do not trouble those who are turning to God from among the Gentiles, but that we write to them that they abstain from things contaminated by idols and from fornication and from what is strangled and from blood" (Acts 15:19–20). That was the extent of their requirements for the Gentile believers.

That is part of why I think we see different types of ministers in the Bible—the church was being formed from very different cultures and belief systems; it is even more that way today.

What about today? Do we have any models of mixing marketplace and ministry? I'm glad you asked—I do have some!

I read the story of Jeremiah Lanphier in the book *God @ Work* by Rich Marshall. Lanphier was instrumental in starting a revival among businessmen in

1857. Chapter 12 of the book describes in much detail what I'm about to briefly cover.

Lanphier was a businessman who was asked by his church to be a missionary to the city of New York. He simply asked the Lord what he should do.

The Lord gave Lanphier simple instructions to have a prayer meeting on Wall Street for businessmen. At first no one showed up, then just a few. Over time, so many people attended that they had to meet at different times throughout the day.

The prayer meetings spread throughout the United States and then to other parts of the world. As a result of one businessman's desire to please the Lord, more than one million people came to Christ through this movement, and many others recommitted their lives to the Lord. God used a *marketplace minister*.

A few years back, there was a college football coach from Colorado who was burdened by the lack of integrity and commitment of Christian men. With the help of other men, he reached out to men in Colorado, encouraging them to keep the promises they had made to God, spouse, family and others around them.

Over a few years of outreach, men filled a football stadium and agreed together to be men of integrity. Over the next few years, stadiums throughout the United States were filled with God-hungry men, pouring their hearts out to God through a ministry called *PromiseKeepers*. Coach Bill McCartney's vision to help men influenced untold millions of men and their families.

McCartney was a *marketplace minister.* He has since laid aside his coaching career to devote more attention to *PromiseKeepers,* fulfilling the Lord's mandate for him.

In the early 1980s the Lord reached out and healed a desperately sick marriage. The couple was in the terminal stages of a cancerous marriage that no one believed could be reconciled. Certainly no one thought they could have a healthy marriage.

The Lord started ministering to the wife. She believed God could do the impossible; He could save their marriage. Then both of them believed it was possible, and they began to cooperate with the Lord to build a healthy marriage.

If that wasn't impossible enough, they had it in their hearts to start an international ministry to marriages. God has moved through them—Michael and Marilyn Phillipps—to establish Marriage Ministries International in more than one hundred countries, reaching out and equipping more than one hundred thousand people each year for more effective ministry by first helping them in their marriages.

Michael is a *marketplace minister.* Before his ministry calling to marriages, he was an entrepreneur. As his marriage was dying in the early 1980s, so were his fortunes. He became bankrupt, but the Lord had given him a gift to create wealth, and that gift didn't go away with his ministry calling.

Michael still devotes about 15 percent of his time to creating wealth through marketplace opportunities. Just in the last few years, he told the leaders of

Marriage Ministries International that he no longer needed to draw an income from the ministry because God had so increased their wealth through marketplace opportunities that wages from the ministry were no longer necessary.

For too long we have assumed that the only way to finance a ministry calling is for other people to fund our vision through the resources God has blessed them with. That is only one model of financing ministry. Another is that God will use the wealth He has helped us accumulate to fund the ministry vision He puts in our hearts. If we have trusted God as our source, using the resources He has already given us is not lack of faith, but rather godly wisdom.

If occupation and ministry can mix, can a pastor or other professional minister receive marketplace ideas to create wealth for themselves or their ministry? Again, the answer is definitely yes.

Mark Gorman is a very effective evangelist and minister of the gospel. For years he has received his financial resources solely from preaching the gospel. A few years ago it was in his heart to give motivational messages to business people. The thought of being a preacher and desiring also to be a motivational speaker frightened him. Some of his closest friends in ministry thought he was wrong about doing it, but he couldn't shake the desire for it.

Through the counsel of his wife and other godly men, he made the decision to devote some of his speaking time to business meetings in which he could do motivational speaking. His humor and delivery style made him an immediate success. Mark now estimates that about half of the revenues he receives are from motivational speaking engagements, and the other half are from typical church functions. It's great that he can raise needed revenue through speaking engagements at secular business functions.

I know that some of you are disappointed with this testimony. You think he is wasting his God-given talents on secular activities; I would say that you are wrong, even if there wasn't more to this testimony.

You see, when Mark speaks at business functions, he asks the hosts who invite him if he can hold a voluntary Sunday church service for anyone interested. Usually they grant his request for the service. Mark says that in the last four years, there have been more than sixty thousand decisions for Christ at those Sunday-morning business functions. More people receive Christ through these business functions than through his speaking engagements at churches.

Marketplace and ministry mix well together for influencing the world for the kingdom of God. But even if the professional minister was given an idea to create wealth in the marketplace solely for his personal needs, that's totally fine. There are many ways in which the Lord may bring wealth to His people, regardless of their position in the kingdom of God.

ALL MINISTRY IS SIGNIFICANT TO THE LORD

Marketplace ministers and their activities, and professional ministers and their activities, are equally important to the kingdom of God.

This seems obvious, but in many Christian circles there is a definite two-tiered system of ministry importance, sometimes described as "clergy and laity." Clergy are the called ministers, and lay ministers merely help them minister. Lay ministers are like apprentices of a trade that can never graduate to the next level.

As a *marketplace minister*, I've occasionally felt the condescending attitude from well-meaning professional ministers of the gospel who hold this view. At times I've felt like what minorities of any culture must have to overcome to accomplish their roles in an environment that is sometimes full of prejudice.

I appreciated what Pastor Rich Marshall wrote on pages 4 and 5 of his book *God @ Work*, which I will quote in the next several paragraphs. He describes succinctly what I'm trying to say. He begins by describing laity and clergy:

> During the years of my ministry, these were the only terms that I knew to describe the difference between pastors and Christian business people. While many people, both in the Church and out of the Church, may understand the basic meaning of those terms, they do not accurately represent the heart of God.
>
> The word *laos* in Greek is the word for "the people," and that is likely the source for the word *laity* or *layman*. The word *clergy* may have its root in the Greek word *ekklesia*. That is the basis for the English word *ecclesiastic*

and basically refers to the Church as the ones called out.

I wonder if *clergy* did not come out of the second part of the Greek word, *Kleisis*, a calling, or *Kaleo*, to call. That would be consistent with the misguided belief that the "clergy" are the "called" and the "laity" are the "people."

But if that is the source of the word clergy, and I can find no other, then it is wrong in its very foundation. For *ekklesia* referred to Church in total as being *the called ones*. You see, I can find no biblical basis for teaching a two-class Christianity of "the people" and "the clergy."

In most cases, when we used the word *clergy*, it was referring to those who had responded to a call of God in their lives and were serving Him in a "professional" capacity. Usually it would mean that they were "ordained" and drew a part, if not all, of their means of livelihood from funds derived through "professional" ministry sources. These clergy types could be pastors, missionaries, church staff, Bible teachers, theologians, leaders in a variety of Christian organizations, or any of a number of other possibilities. But whatever the specific assignment, it was pretty clear, they were "clergy."

"Laity," on the other hand, referred to Christians who were not in the "professional ministry," and the implication was that if they had a call from God, it was not as high a call as the one to "ministry." It did not really matter how committed they were to Christ, how much time or money they gave to Christian causes, or even how gifted they were in the gifts of the Spirit, or in ministry gifts; they were the "laity." In reality, some of these awesome servants of God were much more effective in winning the lost to Christ, in living a life of holiness and commitment to Christ, than some of the "clergy."

Usually in Christian settings, when these servants of the Lord would stand to speak, they would say, "I am 'just' a layman, but..."

Two little words, words that misrepresent God and His plan, have been used by the enemy to bring about the development of a caste system within the Body of Christ—those who are called to "professional ministry" or "full-time ministry": the "clergy"; and those who are not: the "laity." It is my conviction that all of us in the Body of Christ are called to "full-time ministry."

I remember reading this first chapter of *God @ Work* and thinking, *Finally, someone else is saying what I've been saying for more than twenty years, that we are all in the full-time ministry.*

In chapter one of his book, Marshall asks forgiveness for the wrongs committed by professional ministers like him toward ministers like myself in the marketplace. I remember the wave of emotion I felt as God ministered healing to me through those words. As the offended, I had worked through forgiveness toward those who unintentionally put me down in my role as a *marketplace minister*, but when Marshall addressed the offense from the side of the offenders, it moved me immensely.

The other thing I didn't realize until reading the book is how many people were having this same experience, struggling to be recognized and released in their ministry callings in the marketplace. I am excited to see that the Spirit of God is at work to change this man-made religious caste-system of ministry.

Paul writes in Galatians 3:25–28: "But now that faith has come, we are no longer under a tutor. For you are all sons of God through faith in Christ Jesus. For all of you who were baptized into Christ have clothed yourselves with Christ. There is neither Jew nor Greek, there is neither slave nor free man, there is neither male nor female; for you are all one in Christ Jesus."

If we apply that scripture to this context, then we could also say that there is no difference between ministers in the marketplace (laity) and professional ministers (clergy), for we are all one in Christ Jesus. Any distinction made is merely man-made and pride-based.

Marketplace ministers are called of God. They are ministers of the gospel, and they retain ties to the marketplace. Their marketplace ties create influence for the kingdom of God and provide provision for kingdom works. These ties and provisions are then used by the Lord to establish His plans and purposes.

Chapter Six

QUALITIES OF
THE INFLUENTIAL

A sk yourself this question, "Where can I be most influential for the kingdom of God?" When you can answer that question, you know what you should be doing.

Now, ask yourself another question, "How can I be more influential?" Influence determines how many people you will affect.

Perhaps you've heard it said, "Catch on fire, and people will come from miles around to watch you burn." God wants us to catch on fire!

Isaiah 61:1 declares, "The Spirit of the Lord God is upon me, because the Lord has anointed me to bring good news." Jesus fulfilled this verse in Luke 4.

First, He was filled with the Holy Spirit. Second, He defeated the enemy in the wilderness by speaking the Word of God as His weapon. Third, He declared in the temple, "The Spirit of the Lord is upon me, because He has anointed me to preach good news."

Do you know that the same Spirit that raised Christ from the dead dwells in us? Paul writes in Romans 8:11, "But if the Spirit of Him who raised Jesus from the dead dwells in you, He who raised Christ Jesus from the dead will also give life to your mortal bodies through His Spirit who dwells in you."

The same Holy Spirit who dwelt in Jesus dwells in us, anointing us to do the same works Jesus did, and greater.

According to Philippians 4:13, we can boldly say, "We can do all things through Christ who gives us strength." According to 1 Corinthians 12, we know that the Holy Spirit makes available to us all supernatural gifts to help us reach out to the people around us. We have His ability available to us in any situation.

Principles of Living in the Spirit

My wife and I took a walk a few years ago and prayed, and it occurred to me that God had anointed me for living life. He anointed me to be a husband. He anointed me to be a father, businessman and ambassador for Him in the world.

Knowing this changed how I think of myself. I'm more conscious of what I say because I know I am speaking as an ambassador of Christ to this world. I expect God to use me daily. He has anointed me for every aspect of my life. (See 1 John 2:20, 27.) Whatever I am doing, He is with me, teaching me and working through me.

For the last three years I have conducted a Christian men's conference called "Mighty Men of Valor." We usually hold the conference at a resort in central Minnesota.

I remember finishing up an evening session once and feeling exhausted. I had shared a message on sexual purity for men, and half the men responded for prayer at the end of the service. I felt that I had delivered the word from the Lord, but now I was ready to have a very late-night dinner and go to bed.

As we walked out of the conference hall, we noticed three high school girls sitting outside the door listening to the worship band jam. I'd like to think they were drawn to the event, but I think it had more to do with the young, handsome band members who were playing the music.

As we walked by them, the Lord impressed on me to stop and tell them about Jesus. I was tired! I didn't "feel" like stopping, but I obeyed the prompting.

With gentleness, I asked them if they had a personal relationship with Jesus. They didn't. Within a few minutes, I had new sisters in the Lord.

I encouraged them to attend church and read their Bibles. Then, off we went to eat. The Spirit of the Lord is upon us because He has anointed us to preach the Good News.

God wants to use us in the marketplace. He wants us to minister from an overflow of the Spirit in our lives. The following are eleven principles that will help you remain full of the Spirit and His fire if you will incorporate them into your life.

1. Receive the baptism in the Holy Spirit.

I understand that the term "baptism in the Holy Spirit" is not universally accepted in the body of Christ, but whatever you want to call it, experiencing the Holy Spirit is critical for effective ministry anywhere. Throughout the Book of Acts we see accounts of believers who received the Holy Spirit.

After His resurrection from the dead, Jesus told His disciples in Acts 1:8 that when they received the Holy Spirit, they would have power to witness. Acts 2:4 is the first account of the outpouring of the Holy Spirit upon the disciples—one hundred twenty were filled with the Holy Spirit and began to speak with other tongues. Just as Jesus promised, they became powerful witnesses. Peter preached the Good News, and three thousand people accepted Jesus as their Savior.

In Acts 8 we read about Philip preaching the gospel to the Samaritans, and many of them came to Christ. When the apostles in Jerusalem heard that the Samaritans were receiving Jesus, they sent Peter and John to help them receive the Holy Spirit. Receiving the Holy Spirit must have been considered very important if they felt it necessary for Peter and John to go there to make sure it happened.

In Acts 9, after Paul's conversion to Christianity, the Lord sent Ananias to lay hands on Paul so that he would receive his sight and be filled with the Holy Spirit. In Acts 10 Peter was sent to share the gospel with Gentiles, and before they were even baptized in water they were filled with the Holy Spirit and spoke in tongues. In Acts 19, Paul was in Ephesus, and he asked some disciples if they had received the Holy Spirit when they believed.

If it was important to the early church, then it should be just as important to us. These few paragraphs are not meant to be a complete study on being filled with the Holy Spirit. I simply want to encourage you to be open to being filled with and led by God's Holy Spirit.

Luke 11:13 instructs us to ask the heavenly Father for the Holy Spirit in our lives, saying that our request will be answered. Living the Spirit-filled life is living a God-powered life. Why live life any other way?

2. Spend time in the Word of God and prayer, and attend church.

These disciplines are basic to Christianity, and yet, many Christians I know do not spend regular time reading the Bible, fellowshiping with Father God and communicating with Him in prayer, or joining with their spiritual family at a local church.

No book is more important than the Bible. Tapes and books from renowned preachers are helpful to listen to and read, but they can't replace what we find in the Bible for ourselves. It's not what someone else knows that gives us a victorious life; it's what we know for ourselves that counts.

How much Bible reading is enough? Really, the only place you can go to get that answer is from your Heavenly Father. It's not that we have to read the Bible; it's that we get to! God has given us the road map for victorious Christian living. He calls it "The Bible."

It's worth it for us to read the Bible to find out how we are to live here on earth. If you have never read the Bible cover to cover, make it your goal for the next one or two years. Some Bible reading plans take you through the New Testament and the Old

Testament at the same time. I like those plans because they give you God's plan revealed (Jesus Christ the Savior) early in your devotion times. Try it; you can do it!

Prayer is simply conversing with God. What a privilege it is to be able to come right into the throne room of God as His son or daughter. That's the kind of access Jesus gave us with His death on the cross.

When I get up in the morning, I like to sit on the couch for fifteen or twenty minutes enjoying the time quietly before the Lord. Then I read the Bible, expecting God to speak through His Word. I don't claim to be an expert on prayer. I just love to spend time with God, thanking Him and praising Him, worshiping Him, and making requests to Him for my needs and the needs of others.

I also like to listen to what He has to say to me. He says that His sheep hear His voice. I'm one of His sheep, and you are, too.

Prayer is important! When the disciples were with Jesus, they could have asked Him about anything—witnessing, tithing, and so on. They asked Him to teach them to pray. They knew that conversing with the Father was priceless.

Every believer needs to be involved in a local church. Hebrews 10:25 encourages us not to forsake assembling together. Attending church is not just for your benefit. It's for the benefit of others as well. We need one another. We help one another grow spiritually.

Getting involved in a local church is not always

easy. Some people are bound to rub you wrong. There are no perfect churches because people are imperfect, and people go to church. But God commands it because He knows we need it.

Proverbs 27:17 states, "As iron sharpens iron, so a man sharpens the countenance of his friend" (NKJV). No more excuses: Go to church regularly and grow.

3. Be a giver.

Being generous is imitating our Father. John 3:16 states, "For God so loved the world that He gave..." Be generous with what you have: time, talents, and money. Luke 6:38 says, "Give, and it will be given to you. They will pour into your lap a good measure—pressed down, shaken together, *and* running over. For by your standard of measure it will be measured to you in return."

God wants to bless us and make us a blessing to others. He is looking for individuals who are givers, because He provides seed for the sower, the giver.

When Maralee and I were first married, we were literally living on love; all we had was a bed, card table, and a few chairs. God put it in our hearts to give twenty-five dollars monthly to a minister working for Campus Crusade for Christ. We kept that commitment for three years. In all that time, we had virtually no money left over because I was finishing up college, and then starting a business.

You can't imagine his surprise when we told him we wanted to sponsor him. He knew we couldn't have much money, and yet God put it on our hearts to give; we were learning a principle.

You have probably heard people say that you can't outgive God. Well, it's true; just make sure that the One who is leading you to do it is God. Then do it.

A few years ago, the Lord put it on my heart to give a car away. We've done that a few times before, but for some reason, I was having a hard time doing it this time. My flesh wasn't thrilled with the idea, and I wasn't sure it was God.

I decided to set out a fleece as Gideon did. I knew that God really wanted to speak to me in my inner man—that a fleece wasn't necessary—but I just wasn't sure. I told God that if He would tell Maralee that we should give the car away and if she would tell me, then I would do it.

Well, she didn't tell me to give the car away. A few weeks passed, and somebody wanted to buy the car. They had already seen the car and wanted to visit us the next day about buying it. The problem was that I still had that inward witness telling me to give the car away to a particular minister.

Finally I said, "Maralee, has God said anything to you about what to do with this car?" She said, "You mean…like…give it away?" God had been speaking to her, and He had told her to give it to the same minister that He had told me to give it to.

Can you imagine—the Lord told us both the same thing? I guess He is not an author of confusion, is He?

As it turns out, when we called the minister with the news that the Lord had impressed us to give him our car, the Lord had been speaking to him as well. Days earlier, the Lord had impressed this minister to give his old car away. It was the morning of the same day we called him that he yielded to the Lord. He only had one car. He simply said, "Lord, if I have to walk, I'm going to obey You."

Even with both of us dragging our feet, the Lord had it perfectly timed. Be a giver; you can't outgive God.

Generosity gives us influence into people's lives. Our generosity is not to be used as a means of manipulating people or buying their friendship. But, when we are generous with others, we are acting as a channel in which God can show His love to someone.

4. Be a person of integrity.

Integrity is doing the right thing when no one is watching. It's the little things that end up turning into big things.

When I was a little boy attending school, a large television tower fell down near the school. Some construction workers who were doing maintenance on the tower died when the tower crashed to the ground. Some of the students in our school were looking out the window when the tower fell; they saw it happen!

When I came home from school that day, I claimed that I saw it fall, too, but I hadn't. For ten years I had to cover up that lie. My dad would be in conversation with someone, and somehow they would end up talking about the tower that fell. My dad would tell him that I saw it fall, and I would have to lie again, agreeing with him that I saw the tower fall. I was miserable.

Finally, at age eighteen, after I rededicated my life to Christ, I told my dad that I had lied about seeing the tower fall. Even after my confession I had to remind him once during a conversation about the tower that I hadn't seen fall.

I learned a valuable lesson through that mess. Dishonesty has a long tail; it never seems to end. Integrity is being honest about your tax deductions. It's not instructing your staff or family to say you're not there when someone calls you on the phone and you don't want to talk. It's driving the speed limit (I must confess, I'm still working on this one!). It's obeying the hunting and fishing laws when no rangers or other law enforcement officers are around.

Jesus told us in the parable of the talents that in order to be given much responsibility, we must be faithful in the little things. Integrity is doing the big things and the little things correctly. Joyce Meyer says that if you want to be radically blessed, then you need to be radically obedient.

Walking in integrity—when no one can see you—is an act of worship that honors the Lord and strengthens us for greater service to Him.

5. Focus on your vision.

What are you called to do and how do you do it? Without a sense of direction, we're likely to take a "shotgun" approach to life. A shotgun is designed to spray pellets over a broad area, but only has impact for a short distance, often never reaching the target. It's not meant for hitting anything far away and can never be used to hit a long-range target. A rifle, on the other hand, when aimed at a target, is designed to fire a bullet that hits the target even from a great distance.

You may have dreams of doing great things for the kingdom of God. That's good. But most great dreams happen over a great "distance" of time. Write down your dreams, aiming with the focus of a rifle. Ask God to show you what steps to take now to achieve them, and then take those steps.

Joseph in the Old Testament had a vision. His dreams showed him that he was going to be a great ruler. Nobody believed him. He ended up in slavery and prison, but hung on to his vision. Eventually, after many years, his dream came to pass, and he became second in command of all of Egypt.

Visions take time to unfold. Be patient, and trust God to bring them to pass. While you're waiting, however, you must do your part. How? By walking in integrity. Had Joseph yielded to the sexual advances of Potiphar's wife, we may never have heard of Joseph. (See Genesis 39.)

Accomplishing what God puts in our hearts to do also requires us to prioritize our relationships and responsibilities. A prioritized life causes us to make the right decisions in difficult circumstances.

Your personal relationship with the Lord is your number one priority. It should never be compromised. If you are married, your spouse is your second priority, and your children are your third priority. Keeping these priorities properly aligned in the forefront of your decision-making process will help you to make the right decisions. Ministry and work come after the first three. The first three priorities are designed by God to give you strength and a place of refuge in your life.

It is critical to place high value on these relationships and back that decision up with time and effort. There are no shortcuts. They can't be taken for granted.

There are times when changes must be made to realign our priorities as the Lord intended. Part of the reason I made the decision to leave an executive-level corporate position for a lower-paying position with more independence was because my first three priorities were being neglected.

Whenever we make difficult decisions because we want to please the Lord, we can be confident that those right decisions do not go unnoticed or unrewarded by our Heavenly Father.

We must continually resist the temptation to please men rather than God. God's priorities and plans for our lives don't always line up with what others think are appropriate for us.

6. Always be a student.

I've heard it said that instead of trying to improve something 100 percent, try to improve one hundred things 1 percent; that's improvement. Always be a student. Decide you can always learn something; you can always improve a little. Even though I have read the Bible many times, that doesn't mean I can't learn more. When I'm at church, I always open the Bible to the scripture the pastor is talking about because I know I still have much to learn.

My parents are some of the godliest people I know. They are longtime saints who are in their mid-seventies, yet they still tell me that there is much more to know than what they currently know about God. If I live to be one hundred, I hope to have that same attitude.

The difference between a person of average accomplishments and great accomplishments is razor thin. For example, in baseball, an average player hits the ball two or three times for every ten times he is at bat. A great player hits the ball every three or four times for every ten times at bat. A key difference between the two types of players is how much time they each have spent trying to improve their game before they go to bat. The great player will spend just a little more time practicing; he is always a student of the game.

In your marriage and family, always be willing to learn more. According to Jesus, marriages that fail result from hardened hearts: One or both partners stop being teachable. (See Matthew 19:7–9.)

A wealth of material on marriage and family is available for Christians. Take the time to study some of it and get better at being a husband or wife. If you desire to be better in either the marketplace or the ministry, take some time to learn about the area in which you wish to grow. Always be a student; keep growing, and don't grow stale.

7. Don't be jealous of others' success; focus instead on loving people.

Have you ever realized that Jonathan, the son of

King Saul, knew that David was destined because of prophecy to be the next king of Israel, even though Jonathan was the official heir to the throne? Yet Jonathan chose to remain best friends with David.

Celebrate people when they are successful; success is a gift from God. In Christ, your time will come. First Peter 5:6 says, "Therefore humble yourselves under the mighty hand of God, that He may exalt you at the proper time."

I am one of ten siblings. If you are not from a large family, I'm not sure you can imagine what dinnertime was like for a family like mine. Sometimes when I was growing up, it didn't seem like I got enough of my favorite foods.

When dessert was made, I knew there was the potential that I might not get my fair share. We'd jockey for position when the sweets came out because we knew there was only so much of it. I even learned how to make chocolate chip cookies so I could make sure I'd get some.

That may be how it is in some large families, but that's not how it is with God and His family. If He is our source, then He will take care of us. There is an unlimited supply of gifts and provisions from the throne of God.

I love to be around someone who genuinely enjoys being with me. That person strengthens me; he or she doesn't have any hidden agendas. On the other hand, when someone has jealousy in his heart toward me, I would rather not be around that person.

I can feel how they despise me; it's tough to hide.

James 3:16 says, "For where jealousy and selfish ambi-
tion exist, there is disorder and every evil thing."

The law of God's love teaches us to believe in and
hope for the best for everyone. Appreciating others
will give us influence in their lives; they will want to
be around us. In addition, if we are not jealous, we
can learn from those around us who are successful in
business, marriage, parenting and just about anything else. We don't have to compare ourselves with
anyone. We can simply be ourselves, enjoy the relationship and learn from each other.

8. Be courageous for God.

In Joshua 1, Moses died, and Joshua became the
new leader. The Lord told Joshua that He would be
with him, but that Joshua had to be strong and courageous. Four times He told him to be strong and
courageous.

The Lord is telling us the same thing in our role on
earth: Be strong and courageous. There are times
when we must stand up, step out and obey. God will
show you what to do, but you must obey.

When He speaks to us, His voice usually isn't the
equivalent of a neon sign. Rather, it is a still, small
voice. Usually, when the Holy Spirit is prompting me
to tell someone about Jesus, the impression is quite
faint. I'm sure much of that has to do with how
involved I am with what I am doing at the time.

I'm learning to become more sensitive to the
Spirit's agenda and to allow Him to change my
agenda. Sharing Christ requires me to open my
mouth. My lifestyle and actions speak volumes, but

eventually I am given the opportunity to explain why I live the way I do.

It's not our responsibility to save anyone; that's the Holy Spirit's role. But it is our responsibility to "go...and preach the gospel" (Mark 16:15). Many times we are used by God to plant one of many seeds He is using to soften someone's heart toward Him.

I remember having a client in my office once who was about to lose her home because she was unable to pay the loan payments. She was in a tough spot. I wanted to pray with her about the matter, so I asked her if she was a Christian.

Usually I don't ask it quite that way, because in America everyone assumes they are Christian. But this time, that's how I said it.

She responded by starting to say yes, but as her lips formed the word *yes*, she stopped and said, "No, I'm not." Then she switched the subject and asked me if I had ever read the book *Left Behind*. She had just read it and knew that she was not a Christian.

We talked for a while longer, and then I asked her if she thought she would be left behind when Jesus returned. She knew if the rapture of the church were to happen that she would not be taken. That disturbed her, but she was still not quite ready to bow her knee to Jesus.

Near the end of our conversation, she mentioned that her neighbor—who attends my church—had also been sharing the gospel with her. Obviously, God was divinely directing people to share the gospel with this woman.

It's God's will that none should perish, but each of us decides whether or not we will receive the free gift of eternal life. God uses His saints to proclaim the gospel. So be strong and courageous, and do it!

9. Flow under authority.

If you want to be influential with those around you, then you must learn to submit to the authority God has placed over you. Submit to God and obey men. God calls us to submit to men unless they are asking us to do something contrary to His will. If they request us to do something that is against His will, we must not do it and should obey God instead.

The apostle Paul writes in Romans 13 to submit to earthly governing-authorities. Peter tells us to do the same thing. (See 1 Peter 2:13.) For any of us to be influential in the marketplace, we must respect those who have been given authority over us.

The same is true in ministry. If someone has been given authority over you, then you must willingly submit to that person in the area that he or she has oversight. When we have this attitude, God's authority flows down the chain of command right into us. Then we carry within us the authority and anointing of the Holy Spirit to do whatever He asks us to do. If we choose not to submit to the authority God places over us, we remove ourselves from the power that God wants us to have for effective ministry.

I know that I have been successful in business because I don't spend a lot of time trying to change the establishment. I focus on what I can change—me.

10. Do your work with excellence.

Paul writes in 1 Corinthians 10:31, "Whatever you do, do all to the glory of God." He addresses actual slaves in a similar verse from Colossians 3: "Whatever you do, do your work heartily, as for the Lord rather than for men" (v. 23).

If Paul could tell even slaves to do their work with excellence—as for the Lord—I certainly should do my work with excellence as well. If I'm doing it as for the Lord, it's going to be good. Excellence causes us to be influential for the kingdom of God. On the other hand, poor work is a lousy Christian testimony.

In particular, I think one of the poorest excuses for poor work performance is being slack because we are "busy witnessing." You've seen, as you've read this book, that I have shared examples of some of the times when the Lord used me to touch people with the gospel. And don't get me wrong—witnessing is important! But if your work is suffering because of your witnessing, then you are not doing it right.

That's because how we work is a big part of our witness. Day in, day out, doing the right little things when others don't is a huge testimony. Not doing our job well; fudging corners; taking unapproved, long lunch breaks; and other things like that are a bad testimony.

Recently I had to address a bad attitude in myself about my work. The company for whom I sell had put some temporary restrictions on what we could sell. I can tell you that as a salesman, not being able to sell something that people want to buy is hard.

The company gave us a maximum quota that we

could sell on a month-by-month basis. There were guidelines that allowed us to make some exceptions, but very few. I found a loophole in the rules and wrote some additional business.

After a few days, my wife noticed I wasn't acting like myself. She said I was acting like I used to act when I first started in business—business first, then ministry if I had time. As we brought it before the Lord, we discovered I had violated the intentions of the company guidelines. I was wrong and needed to make it right.

First, I called a meeting to inform my staff that I had violated my personal convictions of right and wrong. I told them that even if what I had done was not technically wrong, I believed it was still wrong. I told them if they ever felt uncomfortable with the "rightness" of any decision I made as their boss that they had complete freedom to tell me their concerns.

Next, I called my overseer. I explained what I did and apologized for my attitude. It was simply quiet rebellion.

If we want to be of great influence for God's kingdom, we must have an excellent spirit about everything we do. When we do things with excellence, people notice. Others want to hear about how we have accomplished what we do. It's a perfect time to then give glory to God by sharing with them how He helped us.

Be a good witness for Christ by being excellent at your work. Excellence brings influence.

11. Be a mentor.

Jesus said this a little differently. He said, "Go therefore and make disciples" (Matthew 28:19). Making disciples doesn't necessarily mean making new converts to Christianity. That's only part of it. Making disciples is making followers of the Lord Jesus Christ.

To make a disciple, you have to spend time with that person. Ask God to show you the right people for you to pour your life into. The first people we should be making disciples of are our family members. Our children will respond quickly to the gospel if we start when they are young and if we lead by example.

There is no shortcut to this process. It takes time. The average father spends just a few minutes a day with his children. But it takes more time than that. Ask the Lord for help with this high priority.

Besides your family, who else would the Lord want you to disciple? It may be fatherless young men in your church, your co-workers or people with similar hobbies. People are hungry for the things of God, but they don't always know how to tap into them. Give away what you have learned.

What is most important is spending time with someone and letting that person watch how you live, rather than teaching him or her from a book. Become a friend, and let the process flow naturally.

My dad and mom did a great job mentoring me in the glorious riches of Christ. Here's a poem my dad often talks about that reflects his attitude about mentoring. The poem is "Sermons We See," by Edgar Guest:

I'd rather see a sermon than hear one any day;
I'd rather one would walk with me, than merely
show the way.

The eye's a better pupil, and more willing than the
ear;
Fine counsel is confusing, but example's always
clear.

And the best of all the teachers, are the ones who
live their creed;
For to see good put in action, is what everybody
needs.

In addition, here are five simple steps you can use
that will help you mentor someone…in anything.

1) **You must do it.** In other words, if you
don't live the Christian life victoriously,
why should anyone follow you?

2) **You must teach them to do it.** In order
for you to show an interested person how
to do something, you have to allow them
to be around you.

3) **You must help them do it.** In doing this,
you will need to encourage others to step
out and try it with you.

4) **You must let them do it.** This is their
opportunity to implement what you've
taught them. They do it, and you watch.

5) **You must release them to do it.** Finally,
   you allow them to do it on their own.

I remember when I first learned to fly a small airplane. The instructor showed me how to do it, and then we did it together. After that, I was flying, but he was still next to me. He watched my progress, and the day came when he determined that I was ready to fly on my own.

I'll never forget that day. I didn't know what was coming. We flew a short time together, and then he asked me to land the plane. When I had brought the plane to a stop, he simply got out and told me to take it up again—by myself!

What a thrill it was to fly the plane totally on my own. I had been released to fly.

When we are mentoring or discipling people in the things of God, we need to be willing to release them to the Lord. We don't want to make them followers of us; we want them to be followers of Christ. Encourage them to hear the Holy Spirit for themselves. Release them into their callings.

It takes time for the process of being influential for God to unfold in your life. The first step is simply to say yes to His plan and let Him determine the timing of things.

It's a long journey. Just as we grow and mature as human beings, we grow and mature as spiritual beings. We start out as a baby and progress through childhood, the teen years, and into adulthood. It takes some time, but don't get frustrated. Just enjoy the journey.

Matthew 5:14–16 says, "You are the light of the world. A city set on a hill cannot be hidden; nor does anyone light a lamp and put it under a basket, but on the lampstand, and it gives light to all who are in the house. Let your light shine before men in such a way that they may see your good works, and glorify your Father who is in heaven."

Join me in this prayer:

> *Heavenly Father, help us to be a people of godly influence in the earth. You have called us to be Your light to the world. Teach us to be strong and courageous. We choose to let our light shine into all spheres of influence. Our light will be placed high upon the hills. We will be as lighthouses to the people of the earth. Father, we bring this before You in Jesus' name. Amen.*

Chapter Seven

WEALTH FOR SOWING AND GOING

*P*robably one of the most common frustrations I hear from Christians is that if they only had more money, they would do whatever it was they felt God has placed on their hearts to do. Unfortunately, many Christians are under a large load of debt, or simply have just enough money to take care of their day-to-day obligations.

They hope their situations will change someday. Some even dream of winning the lottery or some other get-rich-quick idea. But their situations will never change if how they think about money doesn't change.

God wants to bless us and make us a blessing in the earth. He wants to prosper us. I've heard it said that prosperity is having enough resources to fulfill God's plan for our lives. It's not just about having all of our needs met. It's also about having enough to fulfill God's purposes through us. And it's about having more than enough.

How do we develop wealth for kingdom purposes? God uses material resources to establish His kingdom through us, so it's worth paying attention to. Jesus talked more about money than any other subject in the Bible because He knows that how we use money reflects what is important to us. Let's begin with addressing a few facts about money from the Bible.

GOD WANTS TO BLESS US!

God wants to bless us, and that includes finances. The Old Testament is full of scriptures confirming God's will to bless us financially. Deuteronomy 8:18 says, "But you shall remember the LORD your God, for it is He who is giving you the power to make wealth, that He may confirm His covenant which He swore to your fathers, as it is this day." Joshua 1:8 says that if we put Him first, He will make our way prosperous and successful.

First Chronicles 4:10 is the popular prayer of Jabez. Jabez boldly asks God to bless him abundantly. Proverbs 10:22 states, "It is the blessing of the Lord that makes rich, and He adds no sorrow to it." Proverbs 13:22 reminds us that a good man leaves an inheritance to his children's children. Throughout the Old Testament, the Lord continually reached out to His people with financial blessings.

What about the New Testament? Does it also confirm God's financial blessings? Let's look at a few scriptures.

Luke 6:38 quotes Jesus as saying, "Give, and it will be given to you...good measure—pressed down, shaken together and running over. For by your standard of measure it will be measured to you in return." The apostle John writes in 3 John 1:2, "Beloved, I pray that in all respects you may prosper and be in good health, just as your soul prospers."

In 2 Corinthians 9:8, Paul states: "And God is able

to make all grace abound to you, so that always having all sufficiency in everything, you may have an abundance for every good deed." Paul writes to the generous Philippians in Philippians 4:19, "And my God will supply all your needs according to His riches in glory in Christ Jesus."

God wants to bless us.

God Doesn't Want Us Consumed by Wealth

As much as God wants to bless us with wealth, He doesn't want us consumed with gaining it. It is not to be our focus in life; furthering His kingdom should be our focus. Proverbs 23:4 tells us not to weary ourselves trying to get wealthy.

Paul clarifies this further in his writings to Timothy. In 1 Timothy 6:9-10 he writes, "But those who want to get rich fall into temptation and a snare and many foolish and harmful desires which plunge men into ruin and destruction. For the love of money is a root of all sorts of evil, and some by longing for it have wandered away from the faith and pierced themselves with many griefs."

Instead, Paul instructs Timothy in 1 Timothy 6:17-19 to exhort the rich by these words, "Instruct those who are rich in this present world not to be conceited or to fix their hope on the uncertainty of riches, but on God, who richly supplies us with all things to enjoy. Instruct them to do good, to be rich in good works, to be generous and ready to share, storing up for themselves the treasure of a good foundation for the future, so that they may take hold of that which is life indeed."

There are many more scriptures telling us that God wants to bless us and that we need to beware of putting our trust in material things. Both are important aspects to be aware of when looking at money. So, assuming that we all agree that God wants to bless us, the next question is, Why does He want to bless us?

I think there are two basic reasons:

1. God is a loving father.

2. He wants to use money to further His kingdom.

We all would acknowledge that God is our loving Heavenly Father. He wants to supply all our needs according to His abilities. Really, there is no limit to what He wants to do for us. If you had a good earthly father, this principle should be easy to understand.

He simply wants to bless us because He loves us. He wants to bless us abundantly enough that we would have enough to pass on to our children's children. Just as I want to give my children as much as they can handle, God, the Father, wants to do the same.

God has also chosen the use of money and wealth as a means to further His kingdom. He wants to bless us financially to help further His own plans. He provides seed for the sower and the "go-er."

The *sower* is the person who gives money to help others fulfill the vision God has put on their heart to accomplish. The *go-er* is the person who is fulfilling the vision God has put in their heart to do.

As sons and daughters of Father God, He expects

us to be good stewards of the resources He entrusts us with. The Lord is looking for good stewards to whom He can entrust His money.

When Jesus told the parable of the talents in Matthew 25, He was showing us that He was concerned that we wisely use the money and talents He entrusts to us.

The Lord gives each of us unique gifts, talents and resources, and He expects us to put them to good use. He ends up giving us more of them when we prove that we can faithfully handle what He has already given us. We all must give an account of how we are using what God has entrusted to us.

The balance we need to obtain when handling money is that God wants to bless us abundantly. He wants us to be wise with how we handle His resources. He doesn't mind us being extravagant; it's not about pinching pennies. He wants His resources to be used purposefully.

Spending money for the glory of God is a form of worship. Extravagant worship is annoying to the religious, but God honors it and is pleased with it. Don't be afraid to be extravagant with money.

I heard a minister share an interesting reflection on the miracle Jesus performed when He fed five thousand people with five loaves of bread and two fish. That was an extravagant miracle from God, and yet, when all the people had their fill of food, the Lord instructed the disciples to pick up the leftover food for future use.

The Lord was extravagant, but not wasteful. That is

how we need to live—generous with others and ourselves, but not wasteful.

God wants to bring great wealth to His people, but He is looking for men and women of faith who have a hunger to see His will accomplished on the earth. Scriptures abound confirming this truth, Proverbs 11:24-25, Proverbs 3:9-10, Malachi 3:10, and 2 Corinthians 9:6-10 are a few examples. The Lord is looking for people who will be good stewards of the resources He puts in their hands.

My wife and I have been married more than twenty years. Over that time, we have had a fair amount of money pass through our hands. As we look back on those years, we acknowledge that we could have been better stewards of that money.

Since graduating from college, we have tithed faithfully to our local church, and given to many other ministries as well. We typically give 15 percent to 20 percent of our income away each year. I just assumed the rest could be spent however we saw fit. That's where we were out of balance.

God doesn't want 15 percent or 20 percent of my life; He wants 100 percent of my life!

The Lord wants us to be completely His. *How we handle money now will determine if we are prepared for God's future plans for us.* He doesn't mind if we have things, but the purpose of wealth is not just to spend it all on our desires. It is also to use it to further the kingdom of God.

Part of furthering the kingdom of God is accomplished by raising godly children. Money is related to this responsibility. Our heart's attitude toward money is reflected in how we spend it as a family. Are we using it in such a way that we are furthering the kingdom of God?

For example, we may or may not further the kingdom of God by what we focus as a family to use our money on. We can choose to send our children to Christian schools or to take mission trips together as a family, or we can choose that these are not important. We can choose to send our children to church camps, or we can choose not to.

Maralee and I are very quick to financially support most of our children's desires to develop spiritually through the Christian activities, music and books they want to spend money on. It takes us a lot longer to make decisions for spending money on things that don't have much spiritual value.

I mentioned in the beginning of this chapter that many Christians want to do more for God but say that their financial situation limits what they can accomplish. The answer is not in the 10 percent that they give as a tithe but in the other 90 percent.

The reality is, most Christians don't even give 10 percent of their financial resources to the Lord's work. The answer to whether or not we will do more for the kingdom of God in the future is in part related to how we handle the money that has been entrusted to us now.

Maralee and I love to be sowers, but we also want to be go-ers. We have a desire to share the gospel with people around our state and nation, as well as the world. *We want to give money into other ministries to help people, but we also want to go ourselves.*

The typical model for fulfilling this desire has been to quit your career, raise support through the help of other generous sowers, and fulfill God's plan to be a go-er. This is a wonderful God given model for ministry. It's been confirmed throughout the ages as a means of promoting the gospel. I fully support this way of propelling the gospel into all nations, but I don't believe it is the only model.

There were places the apostle Paul went where he provided for his own personal needs. He didn't rely on others to give into his ministry; he made tents. It wasn't an issue of pride, of his wanting to be self-sufficient. Paul simply knew that this was the best way for him to reach some of the churches he planted or ministered in. There were other places where Paul received generous financial provision from Christians—like in Philippi, from the Christians there—to provide for his needs as he ministered.

The model I want to address here though is learning how to develop resources that God has given us through our trade to propel ourselves into ministry opportunities around the world. Again, it's not about having an attitude of self-sufficiency, which is pride, but rather depending on God through the resources He has already given us. If we think that it is by our own hand that we can do anything, we will soon become very ineffective for the kingdom of God.

Positioning ourselves for ministry required Maralee and me to take a hard look at how we handled money. Were we using money properly, and were we developing wealth properly? Let's look at these two areas separately, spending money and creating wealth.

For many Christians, the problem is not lack of resources, but poor stewardship that prevents them from fulfilling God's call on their lives.

In 1996, Maralee and I made a career change to position ourselves better for ministry. That change resulted in an initial significant drop in income. Many times, the Lord will have marketplace ministers continue in the direction they are going, but I needed a course correction.

I believe that over time, Maralee and I will be blessed with even more wealth because of our faithfulness to God in this matter of career change. But with our income dropping by more than half, we needed to re-evaluate how we were spending our money. When we had more than enough, it was easy to be extravagant and wasteful. The wasteful part was what needed to be improved.

If you've never had a significant drop in income, you may not be able to relate to this statement. It's hard to adjust to spending less because you have to.

Even in the matters of giving to others, we had to reduce some of our donations. That was hard on my spiritual pride. The Lord was making a course correction in our attitude toward money and it wasn't very much fun at the time.

We found our resources were not enough for us to accomplish what we wanted to do. We had to make some changes, and we began to fervently seek God about what to do. He revealed to us that there were some natural steps and supernatural steps that needed to be taken to get us where we wanted to go.

Those are what I want to share with you now.

My educational and career background is in management and finances, so the natural steps, though hard to make, were easy to see.

First we needed to step back and look at our financial picture to see where we were right at that moment. To do that we had to add up everything we owned, our assets. Then we had to subtract from that everything we owed, our liabilities— and that would be what we had, our net worth.

In addition, we needed to look at our cash flow. How much money were we taking in, and how much were we spending, and what were we spending our money on.

We discovered that we were spending more money than we were making.

You don't have to be a rocket scientist to know you can't do that for too long or you will crash and burn financially. We really only had two options: increase our income or decrease our spending. In the end we did both.

Remember, our goal wasn't just to have a better financial picture. It was to have more resources available to fulfill God's call on our lives. We were serious about this.

We started by reducing our spending. That sounds simple enough, but when you are married, each of you has a different idea about what is important, and what's not.

Maralee and I both agreed it was important to be givers, but it was the rest of the stuff we had a hard time agreeing on. She thinks clothes are important; I think new cars are important. She thinks gifts are an important way to express love; I think a card will do. I think hunting trips build close relationships with male friends; she thinks a barbecue with them would do the same thing.

Actually, she doesn't mind if I go hunting as long as I have prayed about it and get the OK from God. Now that's pressure—"Lord, I want to go hunting, but what do You want?"

We had tried for years and years to develop a budget, but with very little success. For us, a budget was too restrictive.

We needed a paradigm shift—and here it is: *Instead of a budget, we are working on a spending plan. A spending plan determines where we get to spend money. Really it's the same as a budget, but it takes the positive view of allocating money. Because a spending plan is where we get to spend money, we make choices accordingly.*

A budget limits what we can spend money on. In a spending plan we get to do something. In a budget we can't do something. The goals are the same, but the approach to them is different.

I must admit, we haven't arrived in this area yet, but we see light at the end of the tunnel. Together, we are choosing the priorities for what is most important, then following through with proper monetary decisions.

I remember when we first tried to budget our money. It was about eleven years ago. I had just ordered a 9 mm pistol, for home defense of course. Maralee was spending money on areas I didn't think were priorities.

I told her that we really needed to get on a budget because our spending habits were out of control. I was actually implying that *her* spending habits were out of control.

With many reservations, she agreed to start a budget with me. Just a few days later, my new stainless-steel automatic pistol arrived. I was ready to defend our home against intruders of any sort. Honestly, I bought the gun just because it made me feel cool—probably had seen too many cops-and-robbers movies. I really wasn't concerned about home defense; we had other guns—and besides, the Lord was our protection.

Buying that gun blew up our budget plans before they even got off the ground. Maralee considered the gun an unnecessary expense, and I disagreed. I ended up keeping the gun, but destroying any plans for trying to figure out how to have a plan to spend money together.

For a spending plan to be effective, both husband and wife need to come into agreement about what is important and how much emphasis needs to be placed on each area.

By the way, years later I traded the infamous gun for a sentimental gift for Maralee. It was a wise decision that has paid many dividends.

We thought so differently on many points of

importance, so we decided to seek outside sources to help us learn how much money should be spent in all areas of our life. What is a normal amount of spending, we asked?

We looked on the Internet at Crown.org to see what Crown Ministries suggested for general guidelines in a spending plan. This was a helpful natural step to see if what we were spending in various areas of our life was within normal ranges.

Like many Christian financial plans, Crown Ministries suggested that we take our gross income (all money before taxes) and subtract taxes and tithes from that number. The rest would be our net spendable income.

Tithes are taken before looking at spendable income because tithes are not optional for believers. They are just the beginning requirement to get into the game.

I remember one minister describing tithes as "the ante of a godly life." I'm guessing he got that one before he was in Christ—he probably was a former gambler, and God had given him insight into the use of money based on his past experience. When playing poker, before you can even get into the card game, you must put in an ante, a sum of money to start. You can't even play if you don't put the money in.

That's how it is to successfully live the Christian life. You can't live it properly if you don't begin by tithing.

When you have calculated your spendable income, record by categories how you spend your money. "Categories" may include housing, food, transportation, life and health insurance, debt reduction, recreation (including eating out), clothing, savings, medical expenses, miscellaneous expense, and investments. In addition to these, you may have others specifically related to your life, such as Christian education, mission trips, extra ministry giving, and so on.

Some of you may not be able to determine how much you spend on some of these categories, based on your past records. Perhaps you haven't kept good records. If not, you should keep track of what you spend for a few months in order to get a feel for how you are spending your money.

Maralee and I use a computer program for our checkbook, so we can see quickly where we are spending the money. Don't give up on this process because of the extra work in this step. Remember, the goal is to better position you and your family for the future.

After you've categorized your spendable income, you can compare those numbers to suggested guidelines for spending. As guidelines, Crown Ministries suggested that 29 percent of spendable income go to housing, 11 percent to food, 13 percent to transportation, 5 percent to life and health insurance, 5 percent to debt reduction, 8 percent to recreation, 7 percent to clothing, 5 percent to savings, 4 percent to medical expenses, 8 percent to miscellaneous expenses, and 5 percent to investments.

These are only guidelines. If you are married and decide with your spouse that you want to allocate more to savings and investments, for example, then you must spend less somewhere else. They're only guidelines. But in the end, you can't spend more than 100 percent of your total net-spendable income. If you decide that you want to go on regular short-term mission trips or send your children to private Christian schools, then you must decide to spend less money on other categories.

That's the benefit of a spending plan. You can see where you are spending money, and whether or not those spending habits line up with your prayer-focused goals for the future. If how you spend money doesn't line up with where you want to go, then you have the choice to change those habits.

Two helpful strategies to implement when following a spending plan are as follows:

First, *put three to six months' worth of normal spending into savings for unforeseen expenses* such as car repairs, children's braces and so on. These unforeseen expenses occur regularly throughout life, so why not plan for them.

Second, *be wise with the use of credit cards.* Use them only when necessary, or for documentation, but not for impromptu spending. Learn to delay gratification. If you don't pay off your credit-card balance every month, you are not using credit cards wisely.

There is a very important point to remember when developing a spending plan. As a married couple, you must bring your plan before the Lord, and agree with Him about what is best for you. No two plans are the same. We all have unique dreams and situations that require individual choices.

How we spend our money simply reflects where our heart is. Jesus tells us that where our treasure is, there our heart will be also. Choose to create a spending plan that lines up with where you want to go.

Remember, God wants us to live life extravagantly, but not in a wasteful way. A spending plan is simply a natural way to discern whether or not we are living life as to the Lord or not. You may need some course corrections. We still do. We want to be corrected so that we will reach our God-given dreams and desires.

Sometimes changing how we spend money is hard. Often, how we spend money reflects deep heart attitudes of what we put our trust in for security and comfort. In my early twenties, one of my goals was to retire at age fifty-five after which I would really serve the Lord.

As I mentioned in an earlier chapter, the Lord was looking for my full attention to His work right now. He wanted it today, not some time in the future when I felt I had built up enough of a financial nest egg.

We were contributing large sums of money toward retirement. Because of my executive position, I was building a large pension. In addition, I maximized our 401k retirement plan, and when we were eligible, we maximized our Individual Retirement Accounts (IRAs).

Saving for retirement is important, but how we are living now is just as important. My trust in the future was not in the Lord but in my own ability to prepare for it. God leads us to prepare for the future and also keep our trust in Him.

We still save for retirement, but not with the same fervency as I did before. Age 55 is no longer the definite age for us to retire. I don't plan on retiring. If the Lord calls me to do something else, then I will do it, whether that is tomorrow or when I am 75.

We are devoting more of our resources to develop our children as future Christian leaders. We send them to Christian schools, and we often take them with us when we travel for ministry opportunities. We are investing in kingdom activities. It's all about choices.

God has entrusted us with the ability to choose how we spend our time and resources. A spending plan helps keep us on the track we want to follow.

Learn How to Create Wealth

Spending—money going through our hands—is one side of the equation. Income and wealth are the other side—money coming to us and remaining. Now let's talk about wealth and income.

God wants to give us creative ideas for increasing our wealth and income. Part of creating wealth is learning to spend differently, not spending so much on items that are immediately worth very little monetary value after being purchased. It's hard to save and invest money if you've already spent it on perishable items.

Creating wealth also means addressing the income side of the equation. If you have very little income, you can reduce your spending all you want, and you still won't have much left over for accomplishing God's kingdom goals.

Maralee and I wanted to make more time and resources available for kingdom use, but we weren't sure how to do that. When I was in an executive position, I was an employee. I had the resources, but little time for ministry opportunities.

When you are an employee, your time on the job must be devoted to your work. Work is your testimony. It is not a good testimony to witness all day long, and only get half of your responsibilities done for your employer.

We knew that the Lord was leading us to be more active as ministers of the gospel, so we rearranged my career to better position ourselves for that calling.

The Lord put it on our hearts to develop more passive income. "Passive income" is income that comes from sources other than being an employee for someone. *Passive income does not require a regular work schedule to receive the income.*

Maralee and I asked God for help in this area. We felt that He was giving us insight into this area, but it was a new way of thinking for us.

I want to spend some time talking about three areas for creating wealth and income that don't require daily oversight. They are: building a business, investing in other companies, and developing rental properties.

In January 1997 we changed our career path from my being an insurance executive to becoming an independent agent again. Agents are self-employed. Performance is measured by results, not a time clock.

Because I wanted more flexibility in my schedule,

I hired additional staff to help with the day-to-day activities. As I felt comfortable again running my own business. I made a decision to work a four-day week, Monday though Thursday. My wife and I wanted to devote Friday through Sunday for family and ministry opportunities.

The first year we made the change, our production increased more than 10 percent over the prior year. That doesn't make natural sense, but what God is in, He blesses.

Owning a business creates the possibility of more time for other things. It's only a possibility. Running a business can take much more of your time than working for someone else. Each day has the potential for a myriad of problems.

We made it a point to train other qualified people to help us run the business. I am a licensed agent, but I also have four staff who also are licensed agents. If I'm gone for a week or two, I can come back and have virtually no problems to address. That is a tribute to my staff. It is my desire to have each client handled with professional service, though not necessarily directly by me.

A variety of businesses you can own allow you to spend as much time as you want in them. Typically, the more attention you focus on the business, the more successful it will become. The start-up time for most businesses requires extra time and effort, but the long-term rewards for that labor are worth it.

My wife and I pray that our business will be successful and influential for the kingdom of God. We put our hand to the plow, planting and watering, and God causes the growth.

Another way to increase wealth is through investing in other companies. One of the most common ways is through mutual funds. Mutual funds allow you to invest in a large group of companies with a small investment. Investing in more than one company reduces the potential risk of loss from picking a company with poor performance.

Over time, investing money each month causes the little amounts put away each month to become a large nest egg. Time in the market is more important than trying to figure out when to invest in the market. This is typically a good long-term way to invest money.

The federal government encourages people to save for retirement through IRAs and company-sponsored retirement plans. I strongly recommend participation in these programs. The money invested grows without your paying taxes on the gain until you start to spend it at retirement, and sometimes not even then. Building wealth in this way provides future income from small investments today.

Probably the most exciting way that Maralee and I have increased our income and wealth has been through developing land and commercial rental property. We see His hand upon us in this area. We've wanted to develop this form of income for quite a few years, but didn't know how to go about it. *The first step was prayer. We asked the Lord to give us wisdom in this area.* We had the desire, but we didn't have the experience or ability.

The breakthrough started with a seed. The Bible

tells us over and over again that when we give, it is given back to us in greater measure.

Let me share an awesome example of God's faithfulness. We made the decision to buy commercial rental property, but nothing seemed to look right. We simply kept looking. In chapter six I talked about the importance of being a giver. I shared about how the Lord put it on our hearts to give a car to a minister. That was the beginning of our harvest. A few weeks after we gave our car away, I shared with my office staff that we were going to move my office to the other side of the city we live in.

The other side of the city was experiencing great growth, and I felt we would be better off having our business over there. I sent a letter to fifty of my clients to ask them this question, "If we moved, would it affect our business relationship with you?" We didn't want to move and lose too many clients.

Very few said they would leave us if we moved. Just before I sent that letter, one of my clients who was going to get the letter was visiting with a friend. The client was a contractor and owned a bare piece of land in the area I wanted to move my office to. His friend had told him that he should build an insurance office on this bare piece of land and lease it out.

After that conversation, he received my letter about moving my office, and came to see me. He asked me if I wanted to buy his piece of land. He didn't have time to build an office, but he thought I might be interested in the location.

Maralee and I prayed about the piece of land, and

even though we didn't think it was going to be the eventual location for our office, we felt right about buying it. We paid $500 down and began monthly payments on a contract for a deed.

Not long after we purchased the land, the city of Baxter wanted to put a road by our land. They needed this piece of land for water drainage and road right-of-way. The land immediately quadrupled in value. We weren't experts, but we had been praying for God to bless us in this direction, and He did.

Shortly after we purchased the land, we became interested in a commercial building that was for sale in the area where we wanted to relocate our insurance office. It was an old building on an expensive piece of land. It was right on the main route through our city. It required a bigger chunk of cash than I had ever put at risk before.

The building was 7,000 square feet, and my office needed only 1,800 square feet. I had to have at least one other tenant to make it work. Maralee and I prayed about it and had peace that God was in it, but we still didn't know how to make it happen.

I made a list of possible tenants to contact. Then Maralee suggested asking a company called Harmon Glass if they would be interested in leasing from me. They are a large national glass company. When she mentioned them, I got excited about calling them to see if they would be interested.

They were my first call. As it turned out, their five-year lease was going to be up for renewal at the time when I'd have a space ready for them. They had been talking about relocating into the area I wanted to move to, and they wanted to lease from me.

I now had a significant tenant, so we proceeded to negotiate for the purchase of the building. However, we were not the only ones interested in purchasing the building. Someone else had submitted an offer just before we did.

On the day I made our offer, Maralee called me at the office saying she felt she needed to see the inside of the building right away. Maralee had been in prayer that morning and had an urgency to see the inside of the building. She felt it was important for the present owners to meet her.

So we went down to the building and looked at the inside of it and met the owners, a married couple. When it came time to counter an offer, they chose to counter our offer for the building. The prior owners said that the reason they countered to us was not because of our price but because the wife liked Maralee. The Lord had given us favor!

I ended up calling four prospective tenants, and three of them said they were interested in leasing from us. I didn't do any advertising; we just prayed about it. Advertising would have been fine, but we just didn't need to do it.

After we made the purchase, we needed to totally remodel the building. Maralee is the artist of the family, but I had an idea in my mind about what the building should look like when it was done. I wanted the building to have an "up north" look—log siding and posts and a log gable roof with green accent roofing material. I drew it out on a piece of scratch paper for Maralee to see.

On the day I showed her my design, she was going to meet a sister-in-law for lunch in St. Cloud, another city an hour away. After they met for lunch, they drove by a building that looked just like the idea for the building that I had shown Maralee. She borrowed an instant camera and took some photos of the building.

That same afternoon, the man who oversees my agency production was visiting my office. I showed him my plans to move my office, and what I wanted the new building to look like after it was remodeled. He also was going to visit one of his relatives. They decided to have dinner in St. Cloud.

They happened to drive by the same building that my wife had just taken a picture of a few hours earlier. My boss had the same thought about the building as my wife had had. He also took some instant photos of the building.

The next day, within an hour of each other, both my wife and my boss gave me their photos of the same building. It was exactly what I had pictured in my mind. We ended up designing our building from those photos. The remodeling cost was quite a bit more than what I anticipated, but we knew that God was in it.

We now have a building fully leased and generating enough money to pay the bank loan and provide additional income for us. Over the years, the building will be paid off and we will have a generous stream of income from this property. It wasn't our expertise that caused this great blessing to come into our hands. It was simply the hand of God.

All of these examples—developing businesses, investing in other companies, developing rental properties—are ways in which we can develop passive income. These kinds of income don't require us to work ten hours a day, six days a week. They require blocks of time, but then allow for time to do other things, like ministry.

If you are presently receiving all your money from ministry, God may give you an idea to generate passive income. It may be God's plan for you to increase your wealth and income.

I want to emphasize again the significance of working together as a husband-and-wife team to develop wealth and passive income. There is great supernatural power available when we seek the Lord together over a matter. Jesus declares in Matthew 18:19, "Again I say to you, that if two of you agree on earth about anything that they may ask, it shall be done for them by My Father who is in heaven."

Maralee and I are totally opposite individuals. Sometimes we have to work at flowing together. We look at money and financial decisions from two unique perspectives. In the past I would disregard her perspective—it wasn't always logical. Now, regardless of how she comes to her opinion, I value it as a piece of the answer to our decisions.

One time I was very excited about rolling our IRA investment into a new business venture. It sounded really good. It was a new start-up television station for children. When I prayed, I felt good about it. Maralee prayed and didn't get the same excitement that I did.

I didn't want to convince her to come over to my side. I wanted her to hear from God. Because she never had peace about the decision, I informed the broker that we would not be investing our money in this investment. I couldn't give him a reason, only that it we didn't feel quite right about it.

As it turns out, the station never got off the ground. It would have been a terrible investment.

The initial steps for building passive income will likely be in addition to what you are doing right now. In other words, continue what you are doing and add the God-given ideas to the mix. Don't quit your day job. This transition takes time.

If you are an employee, as your passive income grows, you may want to see if you can work a shorter workweek. You may be able to work three or four days a week instead of five days a week. God will give you wisdom and favor in this process.

The Lord knows we want to position our hearts for ministry. We want all our activities to reflect His will for our lives. He has given us wisdom and supernatural favor to develop passive income. This income and wealth will be used to send us forth on ministry adventures and also to help others with their ministry dreams.

Do you see the picture? Our work can be used by the Lord to be a great place of influence for the kingdom of God. In addition, developing passive income can propel us into ministry adventures by creating adequate resources and time to do them.

Just like it takes faith for a professional minister to trust God for finances through contributions and offerings, it takes faith to receive money from our trade, passive income or whatever we put our hand to. Either way, we must believe that God is our source, and no other.

If God is our source, then when we ask Him, He will give us all creative ideas to create wealth and income. If God is our source, then we won't be prideful and tell everyone how wise we were in creating the wealth that God brought to us. I want to be quick to give God the glory for what He is doing.

One other way to provide income for the kingdom of God is through unforeseen sources. Maralee and I were at a minister's conference where the ministry was raising money to expand the ministry across the world. We had already given generously, but wanted to do more. We made an additional pledge of $500, deciding that if the Lord brought us money in unexpected ways, we would give that extra money into the ministry.

It was a six-day conference. The hotel room we were in had a faulty phone and didn't record messages. We were frustrated with the situation, but still nice to the hotel staff, who had tried to fix the phone. When we checked out, they cut our bill in half because of the phone problems.

Maralee and I both knew that the $300 we just saved was part of the unexpected extra money we would be giving into the ministry. It was money we were already planning to spend.

Less than a week later, we were at an outlet mall looking for dinner plates and accessories. Maralee had been looking for a twelve-piece dinner set for almost two years, but just couldn't find the right pattern. She finally found the right set and asked me if I also liked them, which I did. (I say yes to almost every pattern she shows me.)

We decided to buy them and then found out they were on clearance. We were already prepared to spend $250, but were able to get the complete 12-piece set for less than fifty dollars. Again, we knew that we had just saved money for a purpose.

In just a few weeks, we had unexpectedly saved $500 in money we had already made a decision to spend. It was fun to write that extra $500 offering, knowing that the Lord had made a way for it to happen.

Wealth and income, regardless of where God brings them from, should be used for kingdom purposes.

> *Heavenly Father, I ask that you bless us beyond our wildest imaginations. Help us to honor You in all that we say and do. Lord, we want to be a great blessing in the earth. We want You to be glorified through our lives. Make us a people of influence.*
>
> *As ministers in the marketplace, send us forth with the power of the Holy Spirit and provision to accomplish all that You put in our hearts to do. Lord, we declare that Your kingdom will come through us on earth. We will preach the Good News!*

Chapter Eight

END-TIME STRATEGY FOR THE HARVEST

> And from Jesus Christ, the faithful witness, the firstborn from the dead, and the ruler over the kings of the earth. To Him who loved us and washed us from our sins in His own blood, and *has made us kings and priests* to His God and Father, to Him be glory and dominion forever and ever. Amen
>
> —REVELATION. 1:5–6, NKJV; EMPHASIS ADDED

*I*n various Christian circles throughout the world I have heard insightful messages about the fact that the Lord has raised up people in the marketplace and people in professional ministry to establish His will in the earth. Some have used the scripture from Revelation 1: 5–6 to describe those in the marketplace as kings, and those in professional ministry as priests.

If you can only be one, then I think I am a priest in king's clothing. The point being that *God has people in all spheres of influence who need to work together to accomplish His will in the earth.*

Vision for fulfilling God's will in the earth will come to leaders in all spheres of influence: church, government, business, marriage and family, and more. No one person, or sphere, will get all the vision from God. God's plan is for Christian leaders from all spheres to work together with the common purpose of reaching the lost and establishing the Lord's kingdom on earth.

Often leaders from different spheres seem to be working independently of one another, but in reality, the Lord is orchestrating His will through all of them.

In the Old Testament we often see God's plan being implemented through a king and a priest or prophet. At that time, the Holy Spirit had not been poured out on all flesh, and only worked through a few people, usually a priest, prophet, judge or king.

God didn't just speak through the priestly leaders; He also spoke to the king. Often, the king may have had something in his heart that the Lord desired him to do, but God would confirm through a prophet or a priest that it was from Him. One of the benefits of this kind of relationship was that the king could be assured that he was hearing from the Lord about a matter when a priest or a prophet was in agreement about it as well.

In 2 Samuel 7 we are told that King David noticed how nice his own dwelling was and that he wanted to build a nicer temple for God. At first the prophet Nathan told him to do all that was in his mind, for the Lord was with him. But that very night, the Lord spoke to Nathan and told him that David should not build the temple, but that David's descendant should do it. David agreed with the prophet, and eventually David's son Solomon ended up building the temple.

You can see this same kind of benefit with a husband and wife working together in a marriage relationship. The husband, like the king, is responsible for the decisions made in his family. But the wife also hears from God and can give tremendous insight into the heart of God in a matter. Not listening to this counsel creates the potential to miss God's plan. Only a fool refuses to listen to the counsel of his wife.

During different periods of Israel's existence, they have been a rebellious people. When they were rebellious, they ended up suffering the consequences of their actions. It's like driving a vehicle through an intersection on a red light— sooner or later that decision will cause an accident. The only one to blame is the driver who is breaking the law.

EZRA, NEHEMIAH AND JOSIAH

At various times when Israel had been disobedient, they were overrun by invaders and carried off to foreign lands. When they would come to their senses and repent to God for their wayward actions, he would restore them.

The first time, the Israelites were in captivity to the Egyptians, and God used Moses to deliver them and lead them to the land He had promised them. Many years later, the Israelites were in captivity in Babylon. This time God used a variety of leaders to help deliver them and bring them back to their own land.

Two of the leaders who helped lead them out of captivity were Ezra the priest—a descendant of Aaron—and Nehemiah, the cupbearer of King Artaxerxes of Persia. They both found favor from the Persian king and were allowed to return to Israel to rebuild the city of Jerusalem.

I find this story applicable to our discussion on kings and priests because both Ezra and Nehemiah were used by God to re-establish the Jews in Israel. What's even more interesting is that when you read the Old Testament book of Ezra, you don't see much about Nehemiah. What you do see is how the Lord moved through Ezra to re-establish among the people the law that was given to Moses by God.

We see how King Artaxerxes granted Ezra some of his wealth to accomplish the tasks. We see Ezra's faithfulness before the Lord in the book of Ezra, but nothing about Nehemiah's part in the restoration.

If that was all the Scriptures we had on this subject, we would assume that the priest was the only one who had heard from God and that everyone followed this man of God. While it's true that Ezra was a man of God, that the people were greatly influenced by his godly leadership and that the Lord was moving though him, the Lord also was moving through another leader at the same time, Nehemiah.

The former cupbearer to a heathen king, Nehemiah didn't have a priestly anointing—he functioned as a governor. But just the same, God was giving him vision too.

The book of Nehemiah is directly after Ezra in the Old Testament. Nehemiah was a contemporary of Ezra's. Nehemiah had a godly burden to see Israel re-established under the blessings of God. He was fervent in prayer over this matter before the Lord. King Artaxerxes, the same king who granted Ezra's desire to go back to Israel, independently granted

Nehemiah the same request.

Nehemiah's desire was similar to Ezra's, but their strategies were different. Nehemiah wanted to first rebuild the city walls of Jerusalem. He rallied all the people so that each had a share of the wall to rebuild. Because he was governor, he had ultimate authority over the province. Though there was much opposition, the wall was rebuilt in a mere 52 days.

Then we read Nehemiah 7:5 *"Then my God put it into my heart* to assemble the nobles, the officials, and the people to be enrolled by genealogies. Then I found the book of the genealogy of those who came up first in which I found the following record" (emphasis added).

God was speaking to Nehemiah about what to do along each step of the way. Near the end of the book, Nehemiah and Ezra were standing together before the people, declaring God's heart to the people. They were doing it together. They both had part of the vision. They were individually responsible for what God had asked them to do.

As the Holy Spirit inspired them to pen part of God's Word, each of their books reflected what the Lord had done through them individually. A king and a priest were functioning together. Both were significant. Neither was more important than the other.

Let's look at another example, King Josiah. Second Kings 22 describes the rule of Josiah. Josiah was 8 years old when he became king. At age 18 he had ordered the house of the Lord to be cleaned up, an indication that it wasn't really a significant part of the people's lives at that time.

While it was being cleaned, the high priest found the book of the law. King Josiah was obviously curious about it, because he had a scribe read the book to him. Partway through the reading, it appears that the scribe may have read 1 Kings 13:2, in which it was prophesied that a son to the house of David would be born whose name was Josiah. That would have aroused anyone's interest, hearing someone prophesy about you by name many generations before you were born.

We pick up the story in 2 Kings 22:11–13: "Now it happened, when the king heard the words of the Book of the Law, that he tore his clothes. Then the king commanded Hilkiah the priest, Ahikam the son of Shaphan, Achbor the son of Micaiah, Shaphan the scribe, and Asaiah a servant of the king, saying, 'Go, inquire of the Lord for me, for the people and for all Judah, concerning the words of this book that has been found; for great is the wrath of the LORD that is aroused against us, because our fathers have not listened to the words of this book, to do according to all that is written concerning us.'"

Josiah suddenly saw how far away he and his people were from God. In one day, the Lord used him to turn his nation back to God. King Josiah worked with the priests and prophets to rid the country of false idols and anyone who worshiped them. The king and priests were working together.

All Are Anointed to Minister

Today the Lord isn't using kings and priests, but

people who are from different spheres of responsibilities. Kings may be presidents of nations, or a chairman of the board of some Fortune 500 company, or a county sheriff, local doctor, or even an insurance agent. Priests may be apostles over denominations, or pastors of local churches, or heads of parachurch ministries. The key to effectiveness is learning to work together for the common goal.

An important truth that must not be overlooked in linking leaders together is that we are often in different spheres of influence, but we all have a priestly anointing. This is not just for the professional minister; the priestly anointing is imparted to all in Christ.

At the death of Jesus, the protocol for coming to God, and representing God in the earth, was forever changed. Matthew 27:51 states, "And behold, the veil of the temple was torn in two from top to bottom." Before Christ's death and resurrection, only the high priest dared proceed beyond the veil of the temple into the holy of holies, God's presence. This was done only once a year.

The high priest went into that sacred place with a rope tied around him and bells attached to the bottom of his garment, just in case things didn't work out. If the bells stopped ringing, the priests waiting on the outside knew he had died in the Lord's presence, and they pulled him out with the rope.

It was serious business. Priests were not from all twelve tribes of Israel. They were only from the tribe of Levi. There were no others. The priests were to represent Israel before God. They also represented

God to the people.

In the most sacred of all sacrifices, Christ's death, all of that changed. The veil was ripped in two, signifying the awesome fact that all now had access to the heavenly Father through Jesus Christ.

We no longer need earthly high priests. Jesus is our high priest forever! Now we all have equal access to the throne of God. No longer is a priest needed to go into the holy of holies for us, we can go ourselves. No longer do we need anyone to mediate for us, but Jesus Christ alone. As 1 Timothy 2:5 states, "For there is one God, and one mediator also between God and men, the man Christ Jesus."

Now, *all* of us who are in Christ are a kingdom of priests to God. (See Revelation 1:6.) We are a royal priesthood of believers, proclaiming God in the earth. (See I Peter 2:9.)

Jesus represents us before Father God, and all of us in Christ represent God in the earth. We are "Christians," which literally means that we are "little Christs." Christ means "anointed one," so we could say that we are all "anointed ones."

When we look at believers in any sphere of influence, regardless of whether they are professional ministers or marketplace ministers, we must acknowledge that we all are anointed with a priestly anointing to represent God in the earth. We all are ambassadors from heaven.

RESPECTING GOD'S CALLINGS AND AUTHORITIES

So what are some steps that need to happen to cause

leaders from different spheres to begin to strategize together to fulfill the Great Commission? *I think one of the first steps that must take place is for professional ministry leaders to release full-fledged ministers into the marketplace and into all spheres of influence.* If heads of denominations and pastors of local churches begin to recognize and acknowledge ministers operating in the marketplace, more ministers will come forth and minister with greater confidence and Holy Ghost boldness. A new paradigm will be established.

When I first began to step out as a marketplace minister, I greatly appreciated how some of my professional ministry friends helped draw the Lord's gift out of me. I had reached a point in my walk with the Lord in which responding to His leading became natural. I had plenty of opportunities in business circles to speak to groups about business, but now I desired to speak to groups about Jesus Christ. It was a natural growth step for me.

In addition, I had been praying with and speaking to many people on a one-on-one basis about Jesus Christ, so the step to doing these things before groups had now arrived. Over the years, my local pastors gave me opportunities to minister in pulpit situations. I appreciated those opportunities because they were a safe place to develop.

Another minister friend, Mark Gorman, would invite ministers to help him pray for people to receive the Holy Spirit after a message on the baptism in the Holy Spirit. He would specifically point to me and invite me to come up as well.

After ministry meetings that Harold Eatmon organized, he would invite ministers to a room for refreshments. I appreciated his gestures to invite me to attend as well. These types of gestures helped me feel included in the ministry work that was going on. I wasn't a new believer; I had been saved and filled with the Holy Spirit for decades. I was a mature believer. I was ministering in a different sphere, but these professional ministers were acknowledging me as a peer.

Professional ministers have great influence on emerging ministers in all spheres of influence. Pastors in particular can create great opportunities for growth for these individuals. What safer place is there to begin to step out into the gifts and callings of God than in the local church?

As I have been acknowledged as someone capable of ministering to people in church settings or marketplace settings, the Lord's gift within me has intensified. The Lord, through the apostle Paul, imparted spiritual gifts to Timothy through the laying on of hands. Paul reminded Timothy to stir up this gift of God, kindle it afresh so it wouldn't die or fade. *Pastors and other Christian leaders can do a lot to help or hurt in the process of stirring up the gift of God within those around them.*

Before ministers of any sphere can emerge, they must grow spiritually. Pastors and other professional ministers can help greatly in this process. That's what the five-fold ministry is all about—equipping the saints. Very few believers will feel adequate sharing the gospel until they have been grounded in the truths of Christianity and have received the baptism in the Holy Spirit. The best place for this to happen is in local church settings or home cell-groups.

Professional ministers should expect other ministers to emerge from within their ranks. *Growth is a necessary process for a healthy local church, growth in maturity of the believers and growth in the number of believers.*

Just as it's true that pastors and other professional ministers can help emerging ministers, they also can dwarf their growth. Ultimately, no one can stop the will of God from being accomplished in an individual's life but that individual. But why be responsible for hindering the process?

If as a pastor you give the maturing saints under your care little opportunity for growth and hands-on experience in ministry opportunities, you've missed one of your greatest assignments—making disciples. A disciple is not just a follower, but one who learns to do the same things the master does. Jesus said that his disciples would do greater works than He did. A good leader expects his disciples to do even greater works than he has done.

An insecure leader will not allow those under him to excel in their callings. He will always look down on them and see with eyes of doubt and unbelief only what they are now, rather than seeing with eyes of faith what they can become.

The apostle Paul writes in 1 Timothy 4:12: "Let no one look down on your youthfulness, but rather in speech, conduct, love, faith and purity, show yourself an example of those who believe." As mature believers, we must not look down on anyone as they seek to grow and step deeper into serving God, whether they are women desiring ministry opportunities, marketplace leaders or whoever.

We must recognize that God places apostles and prophets in all spheres of influence. If a marketplace apostle is functioning outside the walls of a church building but is every bit involved in setting in place the kingdom of God in his realm of authority, he must be part of the Christian leadership to change that city, nation or even the world. This person, if he functions in the business sphere, will likely not go by the title apostle. It doesn't suit his sphere of influence. But in regard to building the kingdom of God, he is an apostle.

God has a plan for reaching the world with the gospel of Jesus Christ. He gives unique strategies to the body of Christ to fulfill His purpose. Pastors, evangelists, and teachers have part of the strategy, but ultimately the building of the church comes first through apostles and prophets.

Ephesians 2:19–22 states: "So then you are no longer strangers and aliens, but you are fellow citizens with the saints, and are of God's household, *having been built upon the foundation of the apostles and prophets*, Christ Jesus Himself being the corner stone, in whom the whole building, being fitted together, is growing into a holy temple in the Lord, in whom you also are being built together into a dwelling of God in the Spirit" (emphasis added).

It's probably wise at this point to define apostle. I

recently read a book titled *Spheres of Authority* by C. Peter Wagner in which he defines apostle this way: "An apostle is a Christian leader, gifted, taught, commissioned and sent by God with the authority to establish the foundational government of the church within an assigned sphere of ministry by hearing what the Spirit is saying to the churches and by setting things in order accordingly for the growth and maturity of the church."

Apostles build the foundation, and they are listed first in equipping the saints. Because saints still need to be equipped, we know that apostles must still be functioning today. We need them!

It's becoming more and more accepted that the apostles were not limited to the first original twelve whom Jesus picked during His earthly ministry. Just take a look at all the times the word "apostle" was used in the New Testament to know they are important.

When you look up those examples, you will notice Paul, Barnabas, and even James, the earthly brother of Jesus, were listed as apostles. None of these three or others recorded in the Bible were part of the original twelve.

God is causing all the five-fold ministry callings to be recognized in the church today: apostle, prophet, evangelist, pastor and teacher. Just a few hundred years ago virtually none of the ministry callings were recognized as such. Now they are all coming forth in God's intended fullness.

So apostles are in the earth today. Some are being recognized in some circles, others are not yet. Some pastors really function more like apostles. Some marketplace ministers are apostles. When Paul was functioning as an apostle, some of the churches of that time did not recognize his apostleship.

First Corinthians 9:2 says: "If to others I am not an apostle, at least I am to you; for you are the seal of my apostleship in the Lord."

In reality whether or not others recognized Paul as an apostle did not take away from the fact that God called him to be an apostle. But because some did not receive him as an apostle, to them he couldn't function as an apostle. Even Jesus couldn't do miracles in His hometown of Nazareth because they didn't recognize Him for who He was. (See Mark 6:1–6.)

I think that's applicable today. Where our calling is received, we function effectively. Sometimes it just takes some time for change and acceptance to come forth. In the case of Paul, even though not every believer of his time accepted him as an apostle, today we all accept the fact that he was an apostle.

Creating effective strategy will require all of us first to flow "under" authority before we can flow "in" authority. It is critical that we all learn our proper place to function effectively as the body of Christ. Very few people understand authority, and when they do, Jesus marvels.

Matthew 8: 8–10 shows us this: "But the centurion answered and said, 'Lord, I am not worthy for you to come under my roof, but just say the word, and my servant will be healed. *For I too, am a man under authority*, with soldiers under me; and I say to this one, "Go!"

and he goes, and to another, "Come!" and he comes, and to my slave, "Do this!" and he does it.' *Now when Jesus heard this, He marveled, and said to those who were following, 'Truly I say to you, I have not found such great faith with anyone in Israel.'"* (emphasis added).

Jesus equated great faith with understanding how to flow under authority. We need to recognize our places of leadership and learn to flow under the authority given to us in those realms. We ultimately are to submit to God's authority in everything. And God places authority in men that He expects us to follow as well.

Learning to flow under authority means we don't desire to usurp someone's God-given authority. But how do we know if we have the proper attitude about authority, and if we are relating properly to those around us?

In 1 Samuel 15, King Saul makes a sacrificial offering before the Lord that was supposed to be done by the prophet Samuel. Samuel did not arrive on Saul's timetable, so Saul took matters into his own hands and made the sacrificial offering.

God eventually removed King Saul from his throne because he did not submit to God by recognizing the authority of Samuel. His attitude was reflected by actions that twice rejected God's will given to him through Samuel.

"And Samuel said, 'Has the Lord as much delight in burnt offerings and sacrifices as in obeying the voice of the Lord? Behold, to obey is better than sacrifice, and to heed than the fat of rams. For rebellion is as the sin of divination, and insubordination is as iniquity and idolatry. Because you have rejected the word of the Lord, He has also rejected you from being king'" (vv. 22–23).

What displeased God wasn't so much that a king was doing a prophet's job; it was that Saul usurped authority God had given to another. God wanted Samuel to offer the sacrifice, not Saul.

David, the very next king, did things that a priest or prophet was called to do, but he was not displeasing to God in these matters because he did not usurp another's authority. Acts 2:29–30 even describes David as a prophet, even though he also was a king.

Church members try to usurp a pastor's authority by trying to run the local church. A pastor would be usurping authority if he tried to control how a businessman ran his business or how a husband ran his home.

God is looking at our hearts in this matter of authority. The apostle Paul writes, "And be subject to one another in the fear of Christ," (Eph. 5:21). If we have the right spirit, we want someone to do his or her role better. The wrong spirit says, "I can do your role better than you can."

Moses had relatives who came to him with correction. God was pleased with one relative, and Moses made the correction that the Lord brought through him. His name was Jethro, Moses' father-in-law. (See Exodus 18.)

Aaron and Miriam, Moses' older siblings, also brought correction, but nearly lost their lives because of the Lord's wrath against them. Numbers 12:2 describes their conversation when they said: "Has the Lord indeed spoken only through Moses? Has He not spoken through us as well?"

When the Lord heard that, He was not pleased. Because they were offended by a personal decision that Moses made, they felt like they were better qualified to lead the Israelites, but they were wrong.

I don't think Moses made a wrong decision, but sometimes we do make wrong decisions as leaders. That usually doesn't disqualify us for our positions.

Jethro wasn't over Moses in authority, but he came to Moses in humility. He didn't want Moses' job. He simply wanted Moses to do better.

The principle of flowing "under" and "in" authority applies to all our relationships. In the family, the Lord gives authority to the husband. He is ultimately responsible for the direction of the home.

Ephesians 5:22–24 states: "Wives, be subject to your own husbands, as to the Lord. For the husband is the head of the wife, as Christ also is the head of the church, He Himself being the Savior of the body. But as the church is subject to Christ, so also the wives ought to be to their husbands in everything."

The wife honors the Lord with submission to her husband. But if a wife refuses to honor her husband in this relationship, she will find that her children do not submit properly to her co-authority over them. She will reap what she sows. The husband is responsible to back her authority up in their role together as parents.

Ephesians 6:1–3 says, "Children, obey your parents

in the Lord, for this is right. *Honor your father and mother* (which is the first commandment with a promise), *that it may be well with you, and that you may live long on the earth*" (emphasis added).

What goes around comes around. As we submit to our proper authorities, the authority that has been given to us functions correctly. If we choose to reject authority, our own authority is rejected. As wives learn to respect the authority that the husband has been given in the home, the children see her flowing under that authority and learn to respect her authority as a parent as well.

In a local church body, the pastor is given authority over the local flock. As a member of a local church, I am submitted to the pastor's direction for that local church and my part there. If I have a disagreement with some particular pastoral decision or belief, I may respectfully share my opinion with the pastor, but only the Holy Spirit will confirm what the truth is.

I also don't want to try to pull the congregation to my point of view, which would create division. I would be better off quietly leaving than creating division. The best solution is to stay planted and walk in love and respect.

My wife and I are currently Minnesota state directors for MMI. The organization takes a strong stand on divorce and remarriage—that God's plan for a man or woman has always been one marriage for life. Therefore, MMI's interpretation of the Scriptures is that divorce and remarriage is sin. If a couple has done this, they need to repent of that decision to remarry, and not allow another divorce ever to happen again in their lives.

My pastor also takes a strong stand against Christians divorcing, but after a divorce has occurred, over a period of time, he will at times remarry an individual who has been divorced. At times we have different views over this matter of divorce and remarriage.

Even though my wife and I are the state directors of MMI, we have no right to usurp the local pastor's authority in this matter. He is responsible to hear from God and make decisions for members of his local flock. We are not. We may respectfully disagree, but the authority has been given to him in these matters.

On the other hand, when we have an MMI function in Minnesota, even though I am a member of his local church, he does not have the authority to require us to teach something contrary to what MMI has required us to teach. It is outside the realm of his authority.

We are learning to respect the authority God has given each of us. I even told my pastor that if he felt the need to clarify from the pulpit how his view on divorce and remarriage was different from MMI's, he should feel free to do so.

We would not become offended and leave the church. We would still flow together in God's plan and simply acknowledge an area of disagreement on divorce and remarriage.

The time for not walking together as a complete body of believers is over. We need to retain our unique differences and beliefs. It's unlikely that we will all agree on everything, but by walking together in love, leaders from all realms can be more effective working together.

We must respect the authority given to each leader and ministry, and learn to fit where God places us. We might find ourselves living in Minnesota, submitted to a local pastor as one of many members, and at the same time traveling to another part of the world and functioning as an apostle. We can and will have different roles at the same time. Those roles may change over time.

At one time we may be under someone's authority, and over time we may find ourselves peers of that individual.

Barnabas clearly was Paul's early mentor, believing in him when few did. But over time, it's clear that Paul functioned equally with Barnabas in decisions made.

"And after some days Paul said to Barnabas, 'Let us return and visit the brethren in every city in which we proclaimed the word of the Lord, and see how they are.' And Barnabas was desirous of taking John, called Mark, along with them also. But Paul kept insisting that they should not take him along who had deserted them in Pamphylia and had not gone with them to the work.

"And there arose such a sharp disagreement that they separated from one another, and Barnabas took Mark with him and sailed away to Cyprus. But Paul chose Silas and departed, being committed by the brethren to the grace of the Lord" (Acts 15:36–40).

It's unfortunate that they couldn't agree. Mark eventually became useful to Paul. He also wrote one of the Gospels.

Barnabas saw Mark's potential. Paul, on the other hand, saw his immaturity and because of that didn't want him on this particular journey.

But in the end, Paul made the decision that Mark wasn't coming with them, so Barnabas left with Mark. Paul was committed by the brethren to the grace of the Lord and took Silas with him instead.

Our roles can change over time, we must continue to flow in an attitude of humility and let God do the promoting. God will link us to various people at various times to intensify his war strategy against the enemy, Satan.

The Lord is like the Commander-in-Chief, bringing together generals from the Air Force, Army, Marines and Navy to accomplish a specific war mission. Then the generals bring together the leaders under them to execute the plan. The bigger the mission, the more personnel are required. Everyone has a part in the mission. For the mission to be executed properly, everyone must do his or her part.

Just like in the armed forces, where there are different spheres of service and different levels of rank and responsibility, so it is in the kingdom of God. We have different spheres of authority and different levels of authority within the church. We have leaders in every sphere—the church, marketplace, government— and within each of those spheres we have different levels of leaders—apostle, prophet, evangelist, pastor and teacher.

Another similarity is the levels of particular

leadership positions. In the armed forces, we have five-star generals, as well as generals of lower levels. In the kingdom of God, we have apostles over the world, as well as apostles with responsibilities over nations, states, cities and so on.

Ultimately, we need the leading of the Holy Spirit in these things. We need to learn to fit together as the Lord is directing.

Marketplace ministers are part of how the Lord will reach the peoples of the earth in these last days. Business is a sphere of influence that is becoming more and more global. The world is becoming one economy. Influential business people who are first interested in proclaiming the gospel will be greatly used by the Lord in world outreach.

Marketplace ministers will reach people that professional ministers would never be able to touch— Simply because of the unique door that will be open to them because they are in business.

Would you agree with me in prayer for these things to come into place?

> *Heavenly Father, I pray that You will help us to accomplish Your will in the earth. Father, that we all would do our individual parts, that we all would learn to fit together as one body of believers, respecting our unique differences. I pray Lord that those who have been called to lead will come forth into their callings at the appointed time; that Your strategy for the End-Time harvest will be set in place. In Jesus' name. Amen.*

Conclusion

I am convinced that we are living in a period of time when believers in every realm of influence will begin to function as ministers. And because the Lord has given to the church apostles, prophets, evangelists, pastors and teachers, we will see these leadership gifts functioning in the marketplace.

The church is more than a Sunday gathering of believers. It's wherever two or more believers are gathered in His name. Church is "happening" all the time, in every sphere of human activity. The marketplace is no exception. Therefore, we should expect God's gifts to be functioning in the marketplace. "And God has appointed *in the church*, first apostles, second prophets, third teachers, then miracles, then gifts of healings, helps, administrations, various kinds of tongues" (1 Cor. 12:28, emphasis added).

For the transformation of our cities to take place, the marketplace must be reached with the gospel. For the marketplace to be reached, large numbers of Christians in the marketplace must do more than apply biblical principles to their businesses for individual success; they must begin to see themselves as ministers.

Your occupation is your realm of influence; your passion must be ministry—reaching the lost. Let your godly passion drive you. What injustice angers you? Let the Lord use you to help solve that problem. Feed the poor, stop abortion, turn married couples away from divorce, set free those bound by addictions, visit prisoners. Do it all as an ambassador of Jesus Christ.

Isaiah 61:1–2 is still true today for all who are in Christ: "The Spirit of the Lord God is upon me, because the Lord has anointed me to bring good news to the afflicted, He has sent me to bind up the broken hearted, to proclaim liberty to captives, and freedom to prisoners; to proclaim the favorable year of the Lord."

The Lord is releasing ministers of the gospel into every sphere of influence in the earth. If that is you, then you are a marketplace minister.

The Holy Spirit has been given to you to accomplish the heavenly Father's work in the earth. You must open your life completely to Him and be led by the Spirit in everything you do.

Wherever you are, man or woman of God, He is calling your name. He wants you to be a person of influence in the earth. He is equipping you with His gifts and abilities. He will give you ideas to create time and resources to accomplish what He has put in your heart to do.

The eyes of the Lord are still roving to and fro over the face of the whole earth, looking for men and women whose hearts are fully committed to Him—that He might show Himself strong through them.

Don't shrink back, but step forward in faith. The Lord is with you, so you cannot fail. Be patient with the process; it will come to pass.

Paul Gazelka clearly understands that God's people in the marketplace are bona fide ministers. He not only understands it, he lives it. He not only lives it, but he skillfully and clearly communicates it. This is a strategic and timely word for the advance of God's kingdom.

—C. Peter Wagner
Presiding Apostle
International Coalition of Apostles

Marketplace Ministers reveals empowerment for everyone who desires to be a marketplace minister. It is written with prophetic insight and a wealth of experience. Paul is an excellent example of putting the principles he expounds into his life, ministry and business.

—John P. Kelly
Apostle, President, Leadership
Education for Apostolic Development
Ambassador Apostle, International Coalition of Apostles

Paul Gazelka is passionate about the potential of Christian businessmen and businesswomen in the marketplace. He shares from personal experience, believing that God wants to maximize ministry gifts and opportunities in the work place. And he exhorts the reader to dispel common misconceptions and rise to the challenge and callings of God. You can become influential for Christ in the marketplace! This book is must reading for Christians who want their lives to count for Christ. The Great Commission exhorts us to "go into all the world." God has already strategically placed us there. This timely book will help to transform marketplace *workers* into full-time marketplace *ministers!*

—Phil Derstine
Pastor, Christian Retreat Family Church
President, Gospel Crusade, Inc.

When Paul first told me of his revelation regarding marketplace ministry, like most ministers, I couldn't understand how a person could function in the dual role of marketplace and ministry. God used Paul's role in marketplace ministry to open my eyes. My prayer is that this book will do the same for you.

—Mark Gorman
Mark Ministries, Inc.

When I first heard Paul mention *Marketplace Ministers*, I said, "WRITE THE BOOK!" After I read the manuscript I knew why the Spirit of God rose up in me to encourage him. This is *good!*
—RICH MARSHALL
Author of *God @ Work*

Many people are talking today about marketplace ministries. Paul Gazelka is living it out. His book is a combination of his discovering his call to the marketplace and an understanding of the biblical principles needed to undergird such a ministry. I recommend it to those who would extend the kingdom of God into the business world. It will inspire you to serve God wherever you are.
—ALLEN LANGSTAFF
Kairos Ministries, Inc.

There is an awesome move of God happening in the marketplace, and Paul Gazelka gives a true representation of what it means to have your ministry be your work. He is a successful businessman as well as a leader in his church and community. You couldn't find a better representative to write and live this message. Many people talk about integrating their faith and work; Paul Gazelka is someone who has lived it. *Marketplace ministers* is a must read.
—DENNIS J. DOYLE,
CEO, Welsh Companies
President, Nehemiah Partners

Paul's experiences explain how ministry in the marketplace interfaces with ministry in the rest of the church. This book provides an inspiring and useful model for ministers who are finding their way into the effective function of their calling. It will also show many frustrated Christians in occupational roles that their ministry is right where they are.
—DAVID CARTLEDGE
Cartledge Ministries International

A must read for every Christian business person and anyone in the clergy. You'll be inspired and challenged!
—AL LINDNER
Hall of Fame angler
Host of *Angling Edge* television program